Published by:
AcePremier.com Sdn Bhd (829271-K)
N-2-6, Plaza Damas,
60, Jalan Sri Hartamas 1,
Sri Hartamas, 50480 Kuala Lumpur, Malaysia.

Tel: +603-6203 2522
Email: info@acepremier.com
Website: www.acepremier.com

Printed in Malaysia

Edited by: SUSU

978-629-7809-01-4

Cataloguing-in-Publication Data

Perpustakaan Negara Malaysia

A catalogue record for this book is available from the National Library of Malaysia

ISBN 978-629-7809-01-4

CONTENTS

Acknowledgements 10

Preface 13

Part 1: From Deceptive Roots to Collective Defences

1.1 Scam Anatomy and Legal Armour 18

1.2 The Thin Line Between Fraud and Scam 19

1.3 From Street Hustles to Digital Deception 19

1.4 Trust-Driven Scams Go High-Tech 20

1.5 The Technology Trap 21

1.6 The Ripple Effect of Scams 22

1.7 Conclusion 23

Part 2: Unmasking APK Scams

2.1 The Anatomy of Mobile Malware 26

2.2 Tactics and Mindset of Cybercriminals 27

2.3 Risks Driven by Curiosity, Convenience, and Cost 29

2.4 Trusted Sources and Vigilance Against Unofficial Apps 30

2.5 Wedding Invitations and Discount Traps 32

2.6 From Personal Vigilance to Community Empowerment 33

2.7 Collaborative Security Lessons and Future Directions 35

2.8 Conclusion 36

Part 3: The Silent Takeover in a Digital World

3.1 Defending E-Banking from Account Takeovers in Public 39

3.2 Steering Clear of Public Wi-Fi for E-Banking 41

3.3 Dual-Layer Protection for E-Banking 42

3.4 Locking Digital Doors Every Single Time 43

3.5 A Simple Screen Trick for Banking Safety 44

"*Scam-Proof* simplifies cyber safety with real stories and clear tips, helping readers spot scams and stay ahead in the digital world."

Paul Yeo,
Chief Executive Officer,
Confexhub Group

"*Scam-Proof by Ts. Lukas J. Tan* simplifies complex scams into clear lessons, empowering readers to protect themselves and promote digital safety together."

Mohd Yuzairin Md Yunus,
Managing Director,
Akar Indah Engineering Sdn Bhd

"This book is a timely, engaging guide that empowers readers to protect themselves online. With real scam stories, clear advice, and accessible language, it's a must-read for parents, teens, and business owners seeking practical ways to stay safe in the digital age."

Mohammad Effendi Bin Abdul Tali,
Director,
Perak State Development Corporation

"This book offers real stories and practical tips, empowering everyone to stay alert, secure, and scam-proof in today's world."

Akmal Abdullah,
Founder,
Cyverwise Training Solutions

"Lukas' book offers clear, actionable insights — essential for anyone protecting reputation, assets, and clients in today's digital innovation space."

Edward Bigar,
Director

"*Scam-Proof* is a wake-up call for your wallet. Before learning to invest, learn not to get cheated—because financial literacy means protecting your money, not just growing it."

Cheah Zi Kah, CFP®,
Founder

"*Scam-Proof* is a timely, practical guide that empowers Malaysians to stay safe online. With real cases and clear steps, it raises awareness—our best defense in today's digital scam era."

Jason Ch'ng, CFP®,
Founder

"*Scam-Proof* is a smart, practical guide that makes digital safety relatable, clear, and essential for anyone living and transacting online."

Roy Nicholas,
Manager

"We thought we knew!! But do we? A book that has very personal thoughts and sharing through the journey of experience and research of an author on cybersecurity threats and prevention that is suitable for all to stay alert."

Ms. Theresa Chan Meng Yoke,
Senior Lecturer,
Tunku Abdul Rahman University of Management and Technology (TARUMT)

"Lukas's *Scam-Proof* is a clear, practical guide that uses real-life stories and actionable tips to help non-technical readers and communities stay protected from modern scams."

Mr. Vel Muruga,
NCER Entrepreneur Sustainable Transformation Programme (NEST)

"A clear, practical guide by Ts. Lukas that empowers readers to understand, detect, and prevent scams before they happen."

KT Khoo,
Senior Consultant,
Scotwork Asia

"As a programmer, I found this book practical, clear, and essential for anyone navigating Malaysia's growing digital risk landscape."

Mohammed Asif,
Researcher

"An essential read with practical tips and real examples, this book empowers readers to stay safe from today's increasingly sophisticated scams."

Ts. Nikalus Swee,
Workshop Facilitator

"Lukas bridges tech and purpose, turning expertise into impact. This book drives scam awareness—read, reflect, and share for change."

Ismalisa Ishak,
Program Coordinator

"*Scam-Proof* by Lukas J. is a timely, clear guide with practical tips—your essential shield against rising digital scams."

Syazwani Zamri,
Writer

"*Scam-Proof* opened my eyes to overlooked risks. It's more than a guide — it's Lukas's powerful, passionate legacy for digital safety."

Mr. Tan Tee Kai,
Malaysia

SCAM-PROOF

BEFORE IT'S TOO LATE

How to Spot, Stop & Outsmart Scammers

Ts. Lukas J. Tan

3.6 Forging Hack-Resistant Password Locks 45
3.7 Developing Good E-Banking Habits 45
3.8 Conclusion 47

Part 4: Battle Against Invisible Data Thieves

4.1 Trusted Gates Crumble 49
4.2 When Privacy Became a Luxury 49
4.3 Rising Storm in Data Disasters 50
4.4 Massive Security Breach 51
4.5 The Dark Web Déjà Vu 52
4.6 Build Fortress Against Digital Thieves 53
4.7 Conclusion 54

Part 5: Wallets in the Wild

5.1 Evolution of Mobile Payments 58
5.2 The Malaysian E-Wallet Boom 59
5.3 From Cash to Code Payment Revolution 59
5.4 Cashless, Not Careless 60
5.5 The Day Everything Almost Went Wrong 61
5.6 Cashless Transactions and the Art of Deception 62
5.7 The Fake Transfer Tactic 63
5.8 The Parrot That Never Lies 63
5.9 Conclusion 65

Part 6: Digital Impersonation and Its Victims

6.1 Mechanics of Domain and Subdomain Abuse 67
6.2 When Technical Deception Meets Human Trust 68
6.3 The Early Attacks of Domain Spoofing 69
6.4 Phishing's Platform Evolution 70
6.5 Essential Defences Against Web Spoofing 71
6.6 Conclusion 74

Part 7: Email Threats in Corporate Environments

7.1	The Evolution of Communication	77
7.2	Malware Attacks and Operational Disruption	79
7.3	Phishing-Driven Financial Exploitation	80
7.4	Offshore Deception via Legal Loopholes	82
7.5	Proactive Prevention, Rapid Response	83
7.6	Conclusion	84

Part 8: Securing Second-Hand Phones

8.1	The Role of Factory Resets	86
8.2	Understanding Second-hand Phones	87
8.3	The Hidden Dangers	89
8.4	Steps to Perform a Secure Wipe	91
8.5	Real Life Cases and Lessons Learnt	94
8.6	Guidelines and Best Practices	95
8.7	Conclusion	97

Part 9: Digital Hazards of Gambling and Adult Content

9.1	Hidden Dangers in the Digital World	100
9.2	Platform Operations to Deceive Users	101
9.3	The Motivation Behind Visiting Risky Websites	102
9.4	Case Studies of Deceptive Practices	104
9.5	Practical Maintenance Measures for Digital Safety	105
9.6	Conclusion	107

Part 10: Navigating the Maze of AI Scams

10.1	Technology's Double-Edged Sword	110
10.2	AI-Powered Phishing Scams	112
10.3	Deepfake Scams	113
10.4	Vishing Exploits in the Digital Age	114
10.5	Fake Crypto Investment Scams	115

10.6 The Allure of Fake Opportunities 116
10.7 The Malaysian Digital Landscape 117
10.8 Uniting Against AI-Driven Threats 119
10.9 Conclusion 120

Summary 122
References 125
About the Author 135

ACKNOWLEDGEMENTS

This book is the result of not just my dedication, but the collective effort, support, and wisdom of many remarkable individuals and organisations. I am deeply grateful to all those who have contributed their time, expertise, and passion to make this *Scam-Proof: Before It's Too Late* a reality.

First and foremost, my deepest appreciation goes to Dr Jamie Chin, whose spiritual insight and mental clarity offered me grounding and resilience throughout this journey. During moments of exhaustion, doubt, or emotional turbulence, her presence served as a steady light — reminding me to stay centered, intentional, and true to my purpose. Dr. Jamie did more than offer encouragement; she helped me reconnect with my inner strength, reframe challenges as lessons, and embrace silence as a source of wisdom. Her guidance was not just thoughtful, it was transformational — and it became a powerful anchor that kept me balanced when things felt overwhelming.

I am equally grateful to Dr Khalil Zulkifflee, whose sharp entrepreneurial mind and seasoned business wisdom played a vital role in shaping the direction of this book. From its earliest planning stages to its most critical decisions, his insights and mentorship served as a practical compass. He challenged my assumptions, encouraged bold thinking, and reminded me of the value of consistency and clarity in execution. His ability to distill complex ideas into practical strategy helped me move forward with confidence and focus.

Together, Dr Jamie Chin and Dr Khalil offered me both the heart and the hands to complete this work — the emotional grounding and the entrepreneurial structure. Their combined influence extended far beyond mere advice; they shaped the very rhythm and soul of this book. I am forever grateful for their belief in me, and for the light they continue to bring into my journey.

To my incredible tech and business team, your hard work and tireless commitment to this project have been beyond exceptional. From research to design, from coordination to execution, you have given your best. I am also profoundly grateful to my peers and friends in the industry who contributed their expertise, feedback, and encouragement throughout the development of this book. Your insights and shared knowledge have elevated the content, ensuring it remains current, relevant, and practical.

Thank you to:

Shara Wong and Lynn Ho,

Each of you played an invaluable role in making this project a success, and I am honoured to work alongside such a dedicated and talented group.

To the school principals, teachers, and students who welcomed us into your classrooms, your enthusiasm and engagement have made all the difference. It is through your participation that this mission to raise scam awareness becomes not just an initiative, but a movement.

To my beloved family, words will never be enough to thank you for your endless patience, understanding, and love. You are my anchor and my inspiration. Your support gave me the strength to pursue this work, knowing that protecting others from harm is always worth the effort.

Finally, this book stands as a reminder of what can happen when a community comes together with a shared purpose — to protect, to educate, and to empower. Scam prevention is no longer just an individual responsibility; it is a collective mission. I hope that the knowledge within these pages continues to spread, making our society safer, smarter, and stronger.

Together, we can build a future where digital safety is second nature, and scams have no place to thrive.

With deepest gratitude,

Ts. Lukas J. Tan
Founder of OPERiON
Advocate for Digital Safety

PREFACE: A CEO'S SCAM PREVENTION JOURNEY

I am Ts. Lukas J. Tan, the Chief Executive of OPERiON Ecommerce & Software Sdn Bhd. A few years ago, I personally encountered a scam incident where scammers impersonated my company in an attempt to deceive my clients into transferring funds to them. Upon discovering this, I immediately reported the incident to the Royal Malaysia Police (Polis Diraja Malaysia) and CyberSecurity Malaysia. Concurrently, I took proactive steps to raise awareness among those around me about this deceitful scheme.

The ordeal lasted 18 months. Every two or three days, I received calls or messages from victims. Some had lost over RM10,000. Others caught on midway and reached out to confirm. A few were fortunate enough to contact me before any money changed hands.

Initially, I was overwhelmed, and the situation negatively impacted my business. I felt deep sympathy for the victims. To address the issue, we published disclaimers on our website and social media platforms, clarifying the incident. At that time, it was the most we could do.

From this experience, I became proactive in educating my clients about common scam tactics and how to verify the authenticity of information. These efforts bore fruit, as more people began seeking my advice when encountering similar scams. However, I soon realised that merely reporting cases and issuing individual warnings were insufficient to combat the growing problem.

According to Crime Statistics Malaysia 2024, cybercrime surged by 35.5% year-over-year, reaching a staggering 34,532 cases. Among these, e-commerce crimes accounted for 33.2%, while telecommunication crimes made up 30.0%[1]. Through journalistic reports, digital media coverage, and publicly disclosed cases, I have noticed that scams cases are escalating at an alarming rate, particularly within online gaming, such as disguised gaming applications.

Many people lack sufficient knowledge about modern technology and scam techniques, rendering them vulnerable. These experiences have driven me to take more proactive measures.

This anti-scam initiative was born out of the continuous rise in scam cases. I began this mission during the first month of preparing this book, at the same time actively sharing knowledge with primary and secondary schools across Penang. Through the publication of *Scam-Proof: Before It's Too Late*, I hope to inspire more people to join me in delivering these critical insights nationwide, ensuring every community gains the tools to combat scams.

I aim to share my insights and experiences in this book, focusing on non-technical stories, scam techniques, and easy-to-understand graphics, with a broader audience. My goal is to equip readers with the awareness and knowledge to recognise and prevent scams, thereby minimising financial losses.

Scams not only damage a company's reputation and operations but also inflict severe financial and psychological burdens on individuals, families, and society as a whole. The consequences extend far beyond the immediate moment as being scammed can completely alter a person's future. Scams pose a relentless universal threat that transcends age and profession; from tech-savvy young adults to financially established middle-aged individuals and high-income professionals, everyone is increasingly at risk, making digital literacy no longer optional but a survival skill in the modern economy.

---

1. This report covers nationwide data collected in Malaysia between 2021 and 2023 (Department of Statistics Malaysia, 2024).

This book delivers the evolution of scamming tactics, from social engineering to Artificial Intelligence (AI) - driven schemes, while identifying high-risk demographic vulnerability patterns and establishing actionable frameworks for threat mitigation. It also examines how digitalisation and globalisation propel the scam economy, with case studies featuring reverse-engineering criminal methodologies, from phishing lures to romance-investment scams and AI voice cloning, to establish algorithmic models for predictive scam detection. My aim is to help readers develop behavioural awareness, apply evidence-based detection strategies, and act on practical protocols to protect themselves and those around them. Scam tactics are constantly evolving. Our defences must do the same.

Inspired by Sun Wukong's '72 transformations'—a symbol of agile adaptation in the face of danger—we need prevention strategies that are just as flexible. That includes using big data to detect patterns in criminal activity and fostering community-wide awareness to stay ahead of scam operations.

This book is a tactical blueprint for scam prevention for the general public. It reflects my commitment to disrupting scam networks and calls on readers to become part of the solution.

Let's work together to close the information gap, build cognitive immunity, and ultimately co-constructing community defence architectures resilient to organised transnational scamming syndicates.

Ts. Lukas J. Tan

A MESSAGE TO VICTIMS OR NEAR-VICTIMS

If you've been through a scam — or nearly got caught in one — please know this: you are not alone. And this isn't your fault. Scams today are smart and emotionally targeted. In Malaysia, over **RM11.2 billion** was lost between 2020 and 2025 — not because people weren't careful, but because scammers are good at pretending, pressuring, and playing with emotions like trust and urgency.

Many people feel too shy or worried to talk about what happened. But staying silent often allows the damage to go deeper. When someone gets scammed, it doesn't just hurt their wallet — it affects their family, their confidence, their relationships, and sometimes even their peace of mind. That stress can spread quietly through a home, a team, or a community.

Sometimes, simply opening up to someone you trust — a family member, a friend, or a colleague — can lift a burden. Even one small conversation can spark awareness that protects others. In 2023 alone, scam apps (APK scams) caused losses of **RM18.6 million**. These stories are not rare. And that means more people are ready to listen and understand.

This book was created for moments like this — to remind you that your experience matters, and you're not the only one. You're part of something bigger: a shared effort to stay aware, to look out for each other, and to stop scams from spreading further.

Let's grow a Malaysia where we support instead of blame, where victims feel safe to speak, and where staying informed becomes something we do together — family to family, friend to friend.

One voice, one story, one small action at a time — that's how change begins.

Ts. Lukas J. Tan

PART 01

FROM DECEPTIVE ROOTS TO COLLECTIVE DEFENCES

Scams are not only crimes against individuals, they also harm our country and community. By learning about scams and staying alert, we help protect our nation. Every effort to fight scams is a contribution to a safer, stronger, and fairer Malaysia.

1.1 Scam Anatomy and Legal Armour

The first time I started looking into scams, I thought they were just simple lies, something only the gullible would fall for. But the deeper I dug, the more I realised these schemes are far more sophisticated. A scam isn't just about lying; it's about carefully crafting a false reality, one that convinces even the smartest people to make disastrous decisions. The goal is to take money, personal data, or access to something valuable, all while making sure the victim never sees it coming.

The scariest part is that scams evolve with technology. What started as face-to-face cons and fake documents has now become AI-generated voices, deepfake videos, and cloned websites so convincing that even seasoned professionals can't tell the difference. When I came across Malaysia's Penal Code (Act 574, Section 415), it became clear to me that these deceptive acts aren't just unethical; they are crimes with serious legal consequences[2]. That's when it hit me, scams aren't just about morality, they are punishable by law.

Remember: "*Deception is a crime, not just a lie.*"

Every scam fundamentally relies on three unchanging elements: deception, illegal profit, and lasting harm. Deception comes in the form of impersonated bank calls or fake SMS alerts. Illegal profit can be money, personal data, or even access to a victim's device. The harm inflicted goes beyond financial loss, leading to lasting psychological trauma, eroded trust, and persistent shame.

---

[2] Pages 222-224 provide a comprehensive interpretation of Section 415 of the Penal Code of Malaysia, which defines the legal parameters of cheating.

Scammers don't just throw out random bait and hope someone bites. Every trick is deliberate, every word carefully chosen, and every move well-rehearsed. Some victims don't even realise what hit them until it's too late. One thing I've consistently observed is that scams often carry the same traits: urgency, unpredictability, impatience, and a sense of pressure that pushes people to act quickly.

1.2 The Thin Line Between Fraud and Scam

People often confuse fraud and scam, but there's a subtle difference. Fraud tends to be long-term deception operations that may involve corporations or institutions. Scams, on the other hand, are direct hits that are quick, urgent, and psychologically manipulative. They play on human emotions like fear, greed, trust, or even love, forcing people to react impulsively instead of thinking logically.

A fast-talking "police officer" calls to say you're under investigation. A "fake government" email demands payment for overdue taxes. A desperate "friend" on WhatsApp begs for urgent help. These schemes rely on creating panic to override rational thinking. No matter how different they may seem, one thing consistently holds true: if something appears rushed, under pressure, or too good to be true, it's time to take a step back.

1.3 From Street Hustles to Digital Deception

For as long as humans have existed, scams have been part of society. Hundreds of years ago, con artists roamed markets, selling "miracle potions" or claiming to be lost royals in need of gold. Today, those same tactics have gone digital, reaching victims with just a click.

Scams are deeply rooted in human history. Centuries ago, con artists posed as nobles or clergy, exploiting blind trust in authority, which is a tactic mirroring modern phishing emails that mimic government agencies. The medieval forgery of royal decrees shares the same DNA as today's counterfeit e-contracts, exploiting information gaps and human psychology. In medieval Europe, large-scale relic scams syphoned wealth from communities through fake holy objects[3]. It sounds absurd now, but isn't that exactly what modern scammers do with fake investment schemes, promising high returns that never materialise?

Scams don't die; they just adapt to new tools. Once, it was fake signatures on royal decrees. Now, it's cloned banking apps, deepfake voices, and social media accounts impersonating loved ones. It's the same trick, just wrapped in new packaging.

1.4 Trust-Driven Scams Go High-Tech

Scams in Malaysia have evolved to fit the local culture. Years ago, I saw scams built on trust. Take the infamous "monk and nun" groups that roamed Bukit Bintang in 2009. Tourists and locals were approached by fake religious figures asking for donations in exchange for "blessed" talismans. Many handed over hundreds of ringgit, believing they were supporting a good cause — only to discover later that the so-called monks were part of an organised syndicate[4].

Fast forward to 2025, and scams have taken on a new form. Instead of robes and prayer beads, scammers now wear suits and sit behind sophisticated fake websites, promising "once-in-a-lifetime" investment opportunities. One businessman fell for an investment scam that promised 6%-19% returns. He transferred RM166,000, only to realise later that every detail was faked[5].

---

3. The article documents cases of counterfeit relics, including bones misidentified as saints' remains, and their role in diverting financial resources from communities through deceptive practices.

4. Kuala Lumpur fake monks syndicate, where individuals manipulated protective amulets to solicit donations, violating Buddhist ethical teachings (Guangming Daily, 2009).

5. For further context, refer to Oriental Daily (January 27, 2025): A young entrepreneur in Kuantan lost over RM160,000 in savings after trusting a misleading investment scheme promising "up to 19% returns."

This tells us that scammers always play on trust. Whether it's faith, authority, or financial ambition, they find a way to manipulate what we believe in.

The invention of the telephone introduced call scams, specifically fake bank officers demanding payments. The internet introduced phishing emails and deceptive messages designed to steal login credentials. Today, AI has armed scammers with their most dangerous tool yet: deepfake technology.

Imagine receiving a sudden phone call that shatters the peaceful night. Your son's voice, frantic, begs you for emergency funds. Your heart pounds. Before rational thinking takes over, you instinctively act, transferring the money immediately. Later, you realise the voice that mimicked your son's speech patterns was artificial.

AI can now clone voices with frightening accuracy, creating fake emergencies that bypass even the most sceptical minds. By exploiting our deepest emotional bonds, these synthetic emergencies trigger knee-jerk reactions, leaving no mental bandwidth for verification until after financial damage occurs.

Unlike old-school cons that relied on visible red flags, these emotionally engineered attacks represent a dual threat. AI-powered scams don't just leverage cutting-edge technology; they exploit hardwired human psychology. This makes them invisible threats that bypass both antivirus software and common sense.

1.5 The Technology Trap

The invention of the telephone introduced call scams, specifically fake bank officers demanding payments. The internet introduced phishing emails and deceptive messages designed to steal login credentials.

Today, AI has armed scammers with their most dangerous tool yet: deepfake technology.

Imagine receiving a sudden phone call that shatters the peaceful night. Your son's voice, frantic, begs you for emergency funds. Your heart pounds. Before rational thinking takes over, you instinctively act, transferring the money immediately. Later, you realise the voice that mimicked your son's speech patterns was artificial.

AI can now clone voices with frightening accuracy, creating fake emergencies that bypass even the most sceptical minds. By exploiting our deepest emotional bonds, these synthetic emergencies trigger knee-jerk reactions, leaving no mental bandwidth for verification until after financial damage occurs.

Unlike old-school cons that relied on visible red flags, these emotionally engineered attacks represent a dual threat. AI-powered scams don't just leverage cutting-edge technology; they exploit hardwired human psychology. This makes them invisible threats that bypass both antivirus software and common sense.

1.6 The Ripple Effect of Scams

When someone gets scammed, it's not just about losing cash. It's about losing trust in people, in institutions, in the safety of digital transactions.

For individuals, the impact is devastating. Some lose their life savings overnight; others are forced into debt, struggling to recover. Many are too ashamed to speak up, afraid of judgment from family and friends. That silence leads to isolation, anxiety, and even depression.

The ripple effects of widespread scams extend far beyond individual victims. They can erode the foundations of entire communities. Scam victims not only face financial losses, but also suffer tremendous mental pain. For example, after losing their life savings, elderly and teenage victims will have a significantly increased risk of considering or attempting suicide due to financial pressure. Meanwhile, government agencies struggle to keep pace, draining budgets meant to fight cybercrime and diverting millions away from critical public services like upgrading healthcare infrastructure and funding schools.

The economic losses are staggering. According to law enforcement data, Malaysians lost over RM11.2 billion to scams between 2020 and 2025. That's money that could have fuelled small businesses, supported families, or strengthened the economy. Instead, it vanished into the hands of syndicates, leaving victims and society to pick up the pieces.

1.7 Conclusion

The effects of scams go beyond monetary loss. They shake our trust and affect our society. When we stand together, learn from our mistakes, and report suspicious activities, we protect not only ourselves but also our nation. Our collective action makes Malaysia safer and more resilient.

Takeaway: Scam *Dicincang Takkan Putus (Scams may be cut to pieces, but they never stop coming)*

✓ Act Now:

- Report every scam (even minor incidents) to authorities immediately.
- Join neighbourhood watch groups monitoring suspicious activities.
- Support initiatives like PDRM's Semak Mule portal (*https://semakmule.rmp.gov.my/*) for real-time scam checks.

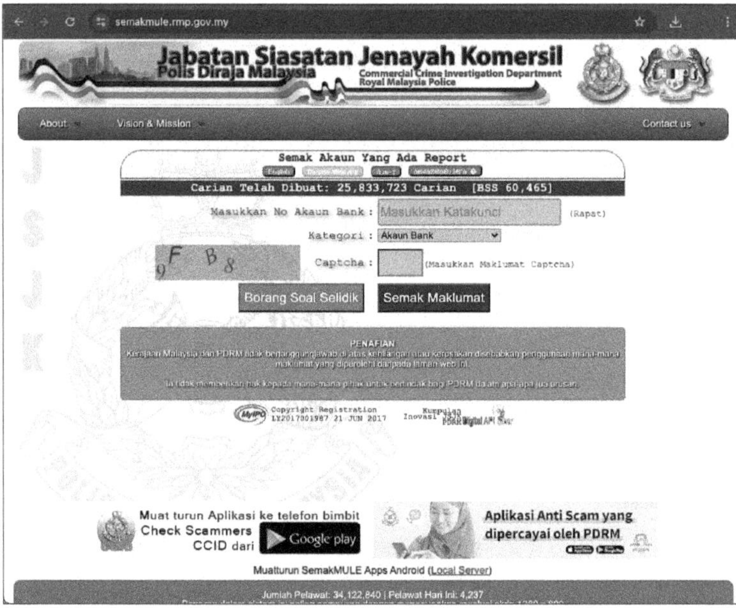

Figure 1.1 Home page of Semak Mule

✖ Stop This:

- Hiding scam experiences due to shame or fear of being judged.
- Ignoring odd requests like sudden TAC code demands from "bank officers."

🛡 Core Defence:

- Scams crumble when victims transform into educators.
- Malaysia's Penal Code (Act 574) empowers legal action, but true protection requires merging the law with communal vigilance, like *gotong-royong* against digital threats.

Scams persist, but united communities wield the cleaver. Forward this book's tips to family group chats; turn your gatherings into scam-awareness sessions. That's why this book isn't just about what happened. It's about what we can do next. The more we understand their tricks, the harder it becomes for the scammers to win.

PART 02

UNMASKING APK SCAMS

In this chapter, we explore how APK scams work and the risks they bring to everyday life. It reminds us that protecting our digital space is not only a personal duty but also a way to help our country and community. Let's learn how to stay safe and support one another.

2.1 The Anatomy of Mobile Malware

An APK scam is a deceptive practice designed to trick users into downloading a malicious application whose primary goal is to access their personal data by requesting permissions that far exceed what is necessary for its intended function[6]. Over the years, I have observed the rapid evolution of digital scams, and one phenomenon that has particularly caught my attention is the APK scam. In my experience, everyday digital communications (whether messages from friends, invitations, or even job offers) can sometimes mask a hidden trap.

An APK scam involves tricking me or someone I know into downloading an application file that appears perfectly harmless but is, in fact, engineered to steal sensitive data. I first encountered the term "APK scam" when I began investigating various cyber threats targeting ordinary users. The process is deceptively simple, like a seemingly innocent link or message inviting me to download an application. Once I click the link and install the file, the application may request permissions that seem reasonable at first glance. However, these permissions are misused to access the personal information I value dearly, rapidly turning what seems like a convenience or novelty into a dangerous gateway for criminals.

The tactics used by scammers are as varied as they are ingenious. Whether through fake wedding invitations or enticing advertisements, their aim is always to lower my guard and build trust[7]. I recall a moment at my favourite

---

6. APK scams involve deceptive tactics (e.g., fake reward apps via SMS/WhatsApp) to trick users into installing malicious files granting excessive permissions, enabling data theft and device control, as warned by Indian authorities and banks (*Kulkarni*, 2024).

7. Scammers exploit trust in social traditions (e.g., wedding invitations) to distribute malware through disguised APK files (*HDFC Bank*, 2025).

kopitiam when, while enjoying a plate of *roti bakar* and a cup of *teh tarik*, I received a warm and friendly message from a trusted contact, perhaps an invitation to a wedding or an exciting announcement. Without hesitation, I tapped on the link. To my dismay, instead of opening a digital invitation or accessing a useful service, I was prompted to download an application file. It was then that I realised the file was no ordinary app; it was an APK that had been tampered with by a scammer. The file requested permissions far beyond what was needed, making me wonder, "Why would an invitation need access to my messages?"

Over time, I have come to understand that the power of an APK scam lies in its ability to disguise malicious intent behind a veneer of normalcy. The file is repackaged to look legitimate, and the permissions it requests (whether to read my messages, access contacts, or intercept one-time passwords (OTP))[8] are the very tools that allow the scammer to breach my privacy. These tactics, which I have documented over time, are not isolated incidents but part of a wider pattern that has affected thousands of users. This realisation has motivated me to educate others and remain ever vigilant in my digital life.

2.2 Tactics and Mindset of Cybercriminals

I have discovered that APK scammers operate by exploiting our natural tendency to trust familiar messages. For example, I have read numerous accounts where a simple click on a link (presented as a wedding invitation, a job offers, or even a cleaner service advertisement) led to the installation of a malicious file. Once installed, these files quickly request access to sensitive parts of my device. Initially, it might seem logical for an invitation app to request minimal permissions, but when I saw requests to read SMS messages or access personal data, alarm bells immediately rang in my mind.

---

[8] The TrickMo banking Trojan exemplifies APK scams' sophistication, disguising malware as legitimate apps (e.g., fake Chrome updates) to hijack permissions (e.g., intercepting OTPs) and exfiltrate sensitive data (*Roviello & Strino*, 2024).

I began documenting these incidents, carefully noting how scammers craft their messages to build trust. They often impersonate friends or reputable organisations, knowing that I, and many others, would be less suspicious when the message comes from a familiar source. Their ultimate goal is to access my personal data (such as OTPs, account details, and other sensitive information), which they can then misuse to exploit my financial resources or steal my identity.

One of the most disturbing aspects of these scams is how they silently hijack personal data. Granting an application the requested permissions effectively opens a backdoor for the scammer. Many malicious APK files are designed to operate in the background without the phone owner's knowledge. Some are programmed to monitor incoming messages in real time, meaning that even if I believe my OTP is secure because it appears on my screen, a hidden process might intercept it before I can use it. In such cases, the scammer gains unauthorised access to my financial accounts.

Moreover, these applications can run covert processes that track my every move, such as recording my interactions, tracking my location, or even sending automated messages to my contacts. The knowledge that my personal data could be silently syphoned away has made me extremely cautious about the files I download.

Equally enlightening has been gaining insight into the mindset of these scammers. They are not merely opportunists, but skilled professionals who invest time in studying human behaviour. They know that we tend to trust messages from familiar contacts and that an appealing invitation or offer can lower our guard. As such, they often mimic the appearance and language of trusted organisations, crafting personal and urgent messages that prompt us to click a link without a second thought.

This understanding has been crucial for me. Recognising that a scammer's primary weapon is our trust, I always verify the source of any message or link before clicking on it. If I receive a digital invitation or an offer that seems unexpected, I take a moment to confirm its authenticity through another channel. This habit has proven to be one of the most effective defences against being lured into a scam. I remind myself that if something feels even slightly off, I must pause and verify its legitimacy. This mindset protects me but reinforces the importance of staying alert in a digital landscape filled with ever-evolving threats.

By understanding both the tactics used by scammers and the mindset behind their actions, I have become more vigilant in protecting my digital life, and I remain committed to educating others about these deceptive practices.

2.3 Risks Driven by Curiosity, Convenience, and Cost

I have often wondered why so many of us, including myself at times, choose to download applications from unofficial sources. I believe there are a variety of reasons for this. Sometimes the desired application isn't available through official channels in my region, while at other times I'm drawn in by the promise of extra features, such as a free premium version or enhanced functionality that is not available in the official version.[9]

There is also an element of curiosity that I, like many others, sometimes feel. The urge to try out the latest trend or a new app that promises to revolutionise the way I do things can be very persuasive. A friend's enthusiastic recommendation, a social media post, or an advertisement that seems too tempting to pass up can easily override my natural caution. Yet, I have learnt the hard way that every time I download an

---

9. *Secure Blink* (2024) warns that users seeking modded apps from unofficial APK sites like spotiplus[.]xyz, lured by promises of premium features and false safety claims, risk downloading malware-infected versions.

APK file from an unverified source, I'm taking on an unnecessary risk. What appears to be a convenient shortcut can quickly turn into a trap that jeopardises my digital security.

👆 Remember: *"Curiosity invites danger; patience protects data."*

I have also reflected on how the appeal of unofficial APK files is amplified by their rapid circulation online. Once one person (for example, me) falls victim to a scam, the malicious application can spread through my contacts without me even realising it. This chain reaction is a stark reminder of the importance of vigilance in the digital world. What makes these files so tempting is their promise of fast access and exclusive offers, but it is these same characteristics that make them so dangerous. Understanding this duality has been essential in helping me adopt a more sceptical and informed approach to the digital content I choose to trust.

2.4 Trusted Sources and Vigilance Against Unofficial Apps

Now, I always download applications from reputable and official sources. If an application is not available on trusted platforms, I reconsider whether it's worth the risk. I recognise the dangers of downloading apps from unofficial sources. Without the safety measures provided by reputable platforms, these files can easily serve as conduits for malicious software. Downloading an application from a source other than an official store is like opening a mystery box. I trust official channels because they come with robust security checks, user reviews, and constant monitoring. In contrast, unofficial sources lack these protections, so when I download an APK file from a random website or an unsolicited link, I'm essentially gambling with my personal data.

One of the most serious risks I've identified is that these files often request permissions that have no relevance to their stated purpose. For instance, if I'm simply trying to view a digital invitation, there's no valid reason for the app to access my messages or contact list. I make it a point to scrutinise every permission an app requests. When access to data or features doesn't match the app's core function, it's a clear red flag. Granting such permissions is like unknowingly handing over the keys to my personal information—opening the door to consequences, such as drained bank accounts, stolen identities, and privacy breaches that may go unnoticed until it's too late.

To protect myself from these risks, I follow several safe practices. First and foremost, I only download applications from official and reputable sources, as these platforms offer layers of security that unofficial channels simply do not. Before downloading any application, I take a moment to scrutinise the permissions it requests and ask whether it makes sense for the application to require access to certain features. If I notice that the requested permissions are excessive or irrelevant, I immediately abort the download.[10]

In addition, I always check reviews and ratings from other users. Feedback from those who have already installed the application provides valuable insights into its legitimacy. If I see multiple reports of suspicious behaviour, I steer clear of that file. These practices have become second nature to me, and I constantly remind myself and others that caution is the key to digital safety.

By combining a healthy respect for the risks with proactive safe practices, I have been able to safeguard my personal data and navigate the digital landscape more securely.

---

[10]. Downloading apps exclusively from official stores and avoiding those requesting excessive permissions are critical to mitigating malware risks, as evidenced by a 2025 campaign distributing malicious APKs via WhatsApp (*Ahmed*, 2025).

2.5 Wedding Invitations and Discount Traps

One of the most alarming examples I came across involved fake wedding invitations. Numerous victims received cheerful messages on popular messaging apps, seemingly from an old friend, excitedly announcing a wedding invitation and urging them to click a link for details. Naturally, I, too, have been tempted by such invitations, especially when they come with a hint of nostalgia and celebration. However, instead of revealing a beautiful digital card, the link led to a request to download an application.

Once installed, the application requested permission to read messages and intercept OTPs, which, if granted, will lead to unauthorised transactions that drain the victims' bank accounts. In 2023 alone, Malaysian authorities recorded 676 cases with RM18.6 million in total losses. By June 2024, an additional 67 cases (RM1.1 million losses) were reported, which were concentrated in Selangor and Penang.[11]

Across borders, I also came across accounts from Singapore where law enforcement dismantled a network of criminals that spread malicious applications disguised as services offering discounted goods or food items[12]. While Malaysian victims were deceived by fake wedding invitations designed to hijack OTP messages, Singaporean authorities were busy extraditing suspects who operated malicious servers affecting thousands of users. Some of these scams even mimicked the style of well-known wedding planners and jewellers, ensuring that unsuspecting victims would never suspect a thing.

These cases have left an indelible mark on me and serve as a constant reminder of the real-world impact of these scams.

---

11. As reported by Malaysian police, 67 APK-related smartphone hacking cases with RM1.1 million losses were recorded between January-May 2024, predominantly in Selangor and Penang, following 676 cases totalling RM18.6 million losses nationwide in 2023 (*Raja Rahim*, 2024).

12. Singapore authorities disrupted a malware operation distributing malicious apps disguised as discounted goods or food services (*Lakshmanan*, 2024).

2.6 From Personal Vigilance to Community Empowerment

Safeguarding my digital life requires a multifaceted approach, which is combining safe downloading practices with continuous education on cybersecurity. My journey into understanding APK scams taught me that basic safe practices must be complemented by advanced preventive measures, and I have adopted a two-pronged approach. First, by maintaining my device with routine security practices, and second, by implementing advanced strategies to stay ahead of scammers.

I perform regular security audits on my device. Every few weeks, I review the list of installed applications and uninstall any that I no longer recognise or use. This habit frees up storage and minimises potential entry points for malicious software. I never compromise on keeping my device updated; I ensure that my operating system and all applications are running on the latest versions and include the latest security patches by reading update notes to understand what improvements have been made. Additionally, I have installed reputable security software that continuously scans my device for any suspicious activity, providing me with peace of mind as an early warning system.[13]

Continuous education plays a vital role in my strategy. By attending cybersecurity workshops, analysing real-world APK scam cases, and collaborating with IT experts, I stay informed about emerging threats like malicious app permissions and OTP hijacking tactics. This knowledge empowers me to identify subtle warning signs, such as suspicious APK file requests disguised as wedding invitations or job offers.

To translate this knowledge into public awareness, I partnered with Malaysian government bodies, such as the Ministry of Education and PDRM, conducting anti-scam awareness talks at primary and secondary

---

13. APK scams distributing malware via fake wedding invitations highlight the necessity of antivirus software and restricted app installations for device security (*The Economic Times*, 2024).

schools throughout Penang starting March 2025. These sessions instruct students and teachers on identifying various scam types and implementing preventive measures.

Figure 2.1 Scam Prevention Talk in SK Saujana Indah

Figure 2.2 Scam Prevention Talk in SMJK Jit Sin

As part of this mission, I initiated the Digitalisation Transformation Summit, held on May 21, 2025 at the PiCCA Convention Centre @ Butterworth Arena. My keynote speech focused on the rising cybersecurity threats facing Malaysian businesses (including SMEs) and offered actionable strategies for adapting to AI-driven technological advancements while mitigating risks. This network has become an invaluable resource, in keeping me informed and helping me continuously refine my defensive measures.

By rigorously implementing basic preventive measures and continuously educating myself about emerging threats, I have significantly strengthened my personal defences against APK scams. Meanwhile, through public initiatives like talks at schools and the Digitalisation Transformation Summit, I aim to build a safer digital ecosystem that benefits the broader community. This dual approach protects my data and empowers others to navigate the digital landscape with confidence.

2.7 Collaborative Security Lessons and Future Directions

Building on the cases and lessons shared earlier, the experiences I encountered — from deceptive wedding invitations to fraudulent advertisements — continue to reinforce the importance of vigilance in the digital space. These accounts not only deepened my awareness but also strengthened a practice I now follow instinctively: pausing to verify before placing my trust. Whether confronted with a friendly message urging a download or an advertisement promising exclusive features, I remind myself that a moment's caution can prevent lasting harm.

By integrating lessons from verified cybersecurity resources, I have built a robust framework for protecting myself. I actively seek trusted cybersecurity news sources and verified updates from official authorities (such as government agencies and banks) to ensure I have the latest information on emerging threats. I also share this knowledge with friends and family, knowing that collective awareness can significantly reduce our overall risk.

Reflecting on how much the digital world has changed and continues to change, I see APK scams as a stark reminder of the delicate balance between innovation and security. While technology has granted me incredible convenience and opportunities, it has also introduced risks that I must navigate every day. Looking ahead, I remain both cautious and optimistic. I know that scammers will continue to evolve their tactics, but I am confident that, with continued vigilance, education, and proactive security measures, I can minimise those risks.

I firmly believe that the future of digital security lies in collaboration among individuals, communities, technology providers, and law enforcement. Every new piece of information, every verified security update from trusted authorities, and every shared experience from fellow users reinforce my determination to stay one step ahead. This commitment will guide me into the future, ensuring that I can enjoy the benefits of technology without falling prey to its hidden dangers.

2.8 Conclusion

Understanding these scams helps us guard our homes and our nation. When we are alert and share what we learn, we make Malaysia a safer place for everyone. Remember, each small step in awareness strengthens our community and contributes to our country's well-being.

Takeaway: Prevention is Better than Cure

✓ Act Now:

- Install apps only from the app store; avoid third-party links even from "friends."
- Before tapping "accept," scrutinise permissions like an uncle or auntie checking out market goods.
- Teach uncles and aunties to spot fake e-wallet APKs.

- If a wedding invite app wants SMS access, cancel it immediately.
- Verify "wedding invites" by calling the groom directly (*Jangan malu-malu!*).

✖ Stop This:

- Downloading "free premium" apps from Telegram channels or Facebook ads.
- Forwarding unverified APK files like a virus.
- Ignoring app update notifications that patches fix security holes.

🛡 Core Defence:

- Treat phone permissions like house keys; only grant access to trusted "tenants."
- Report scam-related incidents to MCMC at 1-800-188-030 with screenshots of suspicious messages, call logs with numbers and timestamps, and APK file samples (if downloaded).

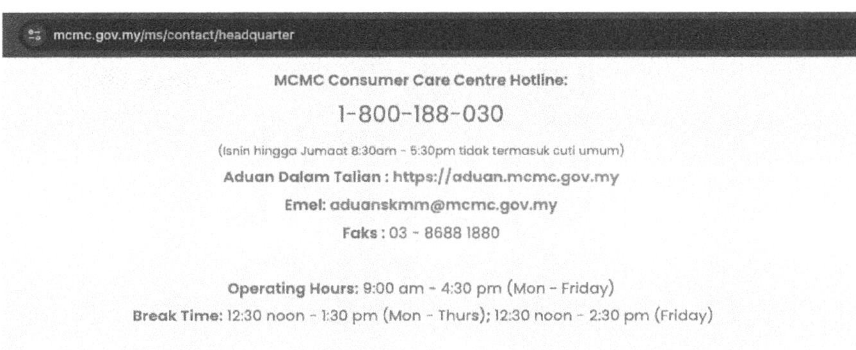

Figure 2.3 MCMC Consumer Care Centre Hotline

PART 03

THE SILENT TAKEOVER IN A DIGITAL WORLD

In today's digital age, managing finances online has become a daily routine for many. The convenience of e-banking allows us to access our accounts and perform transactions from virtually anywhere. However, this ease also brings potential risks that demand our attention. Let's explore practical steps to strengthen e-banking security—simple yet effective habits that can blend seamlessly into our daily lives.

3.1 Defending E-Banking from Account Takeovers in Public

E-banking has revolutionised how we manage our finances, offering the convenience of accessing accounts and conducting transactions from virtually anywhere. However, this convenience comes with its own challenges, particularly the risk of unauthorised individuals gaining access to my bank account—an act cybersecurity experts refer to as a bank account takeover.

A bank account takeover occurs when someone gains unauthorised access to my bank account, often leading to unauthorised transactions or the theft of personal information. I realise this can happen through various means, such as phishing attacks, malware infections, or by exploiting weak security practices.

During my visit to Cambodia, I decided to test the security of accessing my bank account over public Wi-Fi at the airport. Since I was using a Cambodian SIM card, I couldn't receive SMS notifications from my Malaysian bank. Upon arriving in Singapore and switching back to my Malaysian SIM card, I immediately received an SMS stating, "You have transferred RM5,000." Concerned, I promptly logged into my Public Bank account and was relieved to find that no funds were missing. I suspect that if I had logged into my account in Cambodia, my credentials might have been compromised due to potential Wi-Fi hijacking. Although no unauthorised transactions occurred, I took a screenshot of the message and forwarded it to the bank to assist in their investigation and to strengthen security measures.

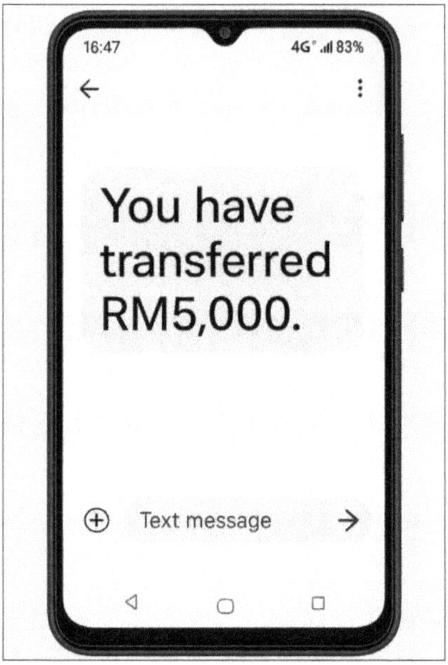

Figure 3.1 Example of the SMS screenshot

Before that incident, I used to think public Wi-Fi was a blessing, just like everyone else did. Free internet at cafés, shopping malls, and airports? To me, it sounded great. But after learning what cybercriminals can do with it, I've stopped connecting to random public networks.

Public Wi-Fi networks, though convenient, are often unsecured. Cybersecurity expert Fong Choong Fook warns that hackers can easily set up fake hotspots mimicking legitimate ones by using names, such as *Free_Public_Wi-Fi* or *Café_Wi-Fi*. These attackers can also infiltrate existing networks to steal sensitive data including banking credentials.[14]

From my perspective, malicious actors can harvest critical digital assets ranging from banking credentials (including passwords and login details) to social media account access and financial instruments, such

---

14. Based on an interview with Fong reported by Muhammad Saufi Hassan dan Ekhwan Haque Fazlul Haque, *Harian Metro*, February 23, 2020.

as credit card numbers. This data extraction extends to personal digital footprints, encompassing private files, contact networks, and email account privileges.

To me, using unsecured Wi-Fi to check my bank balance is like shouting my ATM PIN in a crowded LRT. Hackers don't need fancy tools, just a cheap router and a hidden laptop to steal my passwords, card details, and even my WhatsApp chats.

I believe this threat is real and happening now. Hackers have already targeted big companies, forcing them to pay millions to restore their systems. If these companies with huge security budgets can be hacked, ordinary people like us face even bigger risks if we don't take safety measures.

In my daily life, managing finances online has become second nature. The convenience of accessing my bank accounts from anywhere, at any time, feels unparalleled. However, this convenience also brings about potential risks that demand my vigilance. Let's explore practical steps I take to strengthen my e-banking security, simple yet effective habits that seamlessly integrate into my daily routine.

3.2 Steering Clear of Public Wi-Fi for E-Banking

I think of public Wi-Fi as a food stall run by strangers. Sure, it's tempting, but would I hand my wallet to the uncle or auntie beside me?

This digital risk manifests when I log into my bank account on public Wi-Fi, essentially allowing strangers to 'peek' into my digital wallet. Whether I'm at home, in the office, or a public space, all my online activities pass through a router, which logs my network traffic, including visited websites and data transfers. While encryption on routers offers some protection, I realise even if the café owner isn't a scammer, hackers can hack the router itself. Once they're in, they'll see everything—my banks' login, my online shopping records, even that embarrassing web page search history. This vulnerability isn't necessarily due to the router owner's negligence but can result from external attacks.

Therefore, I recommend avoiding public Wi-Fi when accessing your e-banking accounts and using mobile data instead. If I absolutely need to connect in high-risk areas like malls or airports, I always activate a VPN first. It creates an encrypted tunnel for my internet traffic, adding a crucial layer of protection.

3.3 Dual-Layer Protection for E-Banking

Think about my everyday browser as a crowded *pasar malam* (night market). It's lively, with various stalls (websites) vying for my attention. While it's convenient to have everything in one place, I realise it also means my browser is handling a lot of information, such as cookies, ads, and tabs from dodgy sites, simultaneously.

By dedicating a separate browser solely for e-banking, I'm essentially creating a quiet, secure room away from the crowded market. This isolation minimises the risk of cross-site tracking and reduces the chances of malicious scripts interfering with my banking sessions.

While dedicated browsers provide essential isolation, combining them with incognito mode creates layered protection. In my practice, using Google Chrome with incognito mode for bank transfers adds an extra safeguard alongside browser separation. This dual approach, while not completely foolproof, significantly reduces my exposure by isolating financial activities in a dedicated browser and enabling added protection—compared to using a single browser without privacy mode.

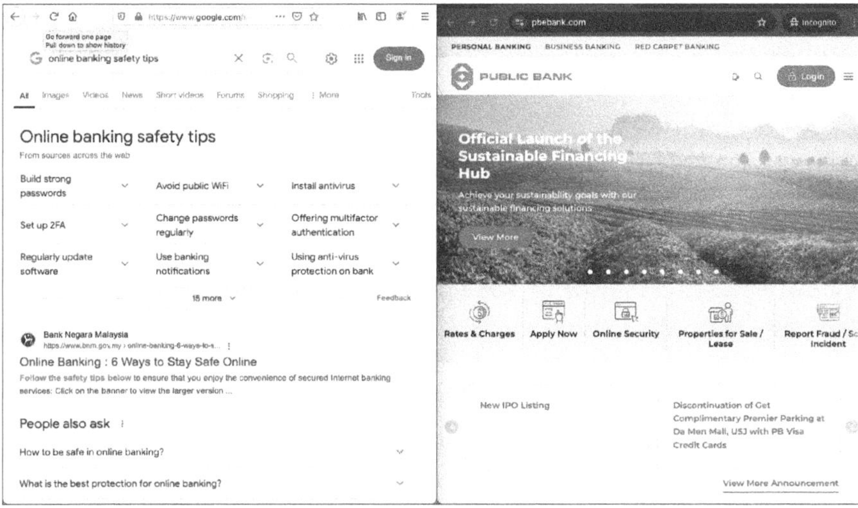

Figure 3.2 Example of daily browsing vs. separate browser with incognito mode for e-banking

For instance, I maintain daily browsing on Google Chrome while reserving Mozilla Firefox or Microsoft Edge for e-banking to achieve critical separation. This strategic isolation ensures my banking sessions remain walled off from regular online activities, much like keeping financial documents in a fireproof safe within a guarded office.

By adopting this simple habit, I feel I'm taking a proactive step in safeguarding my financial information. It's like choosing to discuss sensitive matters in a quiet, private space rather than in the middle of a crowded street. In the ever-evolving landscape of online security, I believe such measures can make a significant difference in protecting my hard-earned money.

3.4 Locking Digital Doors Every Single Time

As someone who banks online regularly, I've realised that logging out properly matters—whether I'm on my personal laptop or a shared computer. Even my devices aren't foolproof. If I forget to log out, anyone with temporary access, like a family member, a friend who borrows my laptop, or even a snooping colleague, can access my account unnoticed.

I find incognito mode to be handy. It stops my browser from saving passwords or history, like wiping my footprints after walking. But the problem here is that incognito mode doesn't automatically log me out. An open banking session, even on my private device, feels like leaving my house keys dangling in the door. That's why I make it a habit to manually log out every single time, no exceptions.

My rule remains straightforward: combining incognito mode with manual logouts cuts risks, such as cached data leaks or prying eyes. For peace of mind, I never skip these twin safeguards when banking online. This dual approach mirrors locking my door and sliding the deadbolt before leaving home, two essential steps that jointly block unauthorised access.

Remember: *"Log out like you lock out."*

But security doesn't stop there; it requires ongoing vigilance. Similar to how I'd also check window latches after securing doors, online banking needs extra layers of simple precautions.

3.5 A Simple Screen Trick for Banking Safety

Most users overlook a straightforward safety step, but I avoid full-screen mode during online banking. Cybercriminals often plant spyware through seemingly legitimate websites. Once installed, this malware waits for me to access banking portals. Hackers program these tools to automatically capture screenshots based on standard screen sizes. Simply making my browser window smaller than usual (e.g., 80% of full screen) can turn their stolen screenshots into something blurry and useless. This quick adjustment takes seconds but provides an additional layer of security.

Adjusting my banking window size acts like closing curtains: it blocks outsiders from seeing inside my house and denies criminals a clear visual of my financial activities.

3.6 Forging Hack-Resistant Password Locks

I always think of my password as the lock on my front door. A flimsy lock like "Password123" or my birthday is easy to pick. Here's how I fortify it:

(a) Mix characters: I use a combination of uppercase and lowercase letters, numbers, and special symbols. For instance, I turn '*lepak*' into '*L3p@k_Mamak!*' (But I don't use this exact one, lah!). This complexity makes it harder for attackers to guess.

(b) Avoid personal info: I steer clear of easily guessable details like my name, birthdate, or simple sequences. Scammers can find these from social media profiles, making such passwords vulnerable.

(c) Change regularly: I rotate passwords like my curry recipe; updating every three months adds an extra layer of security[15].

A strong password is my line of defence against unauthorised access. By implementing these practices, I significantly reduce the risk of compromising my personal and financial information.

3.7 Developing Good E-Banking Habits

Just as I have habits like locking my doors at night, I cultivate good e-banking practices:

(a) Always Verify the Bank's Official Website: Before entering my login details, I ensure I'm on the bank's legitimate website. I type the URL directly into my browser and look for "https" at the

---

[15] Hui (2023) recommends using complex, non-personal passwords and updating them regularly to reduce the risk of cyber threats.

beginning of the address, indicating a secure connection. This simple step helps me avoid falling victim to fake websites designed to steal my information.

(b) **Confirm My Personal Security Image or Phrase:** Many banks use a Personal Identification Phrase (PIP) or image as an extra layer of security. If I notice anything unusual about my PIP, such as a different image or phrase, I do not proceed with entering my password. Instead, I contact my bank immediately to report the discrepancy.

(c) **Keep My Account Details Confidential:** I keep my account information private. I never share my business account numbers, user IDs, passwords, or answers to security questions with anyone, even if they claim to be from the bank. I remember that legitimate bank representatives will never ask for my password.

(d) **Review Transaction Details Carefully:** Before authorising any transactions through the bank's website or app, I take a moment to double-check the details. I ensure the recipient's information and the transaction amount are correct. This habit helps me avoid mistakes and unauthorised transfers.

(e) **Regularly Monitor My Account:** I make it a routine to check my account balance and statements. I look out for any unauthorised transactions or unusual activity. If something doesn't seem right, I contact my bank immediately. Prompt action can make a significant difference in resolving issues quickly.

(f) **Stay Updated with the Bank's Security Centre:** Banks often provide resources and updates about the latest scams and security tips. I regularly visit my bank's security centre to stay informed and recognise potential threats before they affect me.

By incorporating these practices into my e-banking routine, I enjoy the convenience of digital finance with greater peace of mind. I stay vigilant and proactive to keep my financial information secure.

3.8 Conclusion

In the realm of online banking, consistent vigilance is our strongest ally. By integrating the above habits into our daily routine, we safeguard our financial assets and contribute to a safer digital banking environment for everyone. Remember, in the digital world, small, consistent actions lead to long-term security.

Takeaway: *Sikit-sikit, Lama-lama Jadi Selamat*

✓ Act Now:

- Switch to mobile data when banking in public spaces.
- Your telco's 4G is safer than "Free_Wi-Fi."
- Bookmark your bank's official login page (e.g., *https://maybank2u.com.my*) to avoid typos that lead to fake sites.

✖ Stop This:

- Rushing to claim "limited-time offers" via public Wi-Fi.
- Entering banking passwords while connected to public networks, even for "urgent" transactions.

🛡 Core Defence:

True security respects the practical needs of Malaysians while ensuring strong protection:

- *Kiasu* Wisdom: Use bank apps' built-in security (like CIMB's SecureTAC).
- *Kiasi* Vigilance: Always have a smaller banking window size and double-check URLs before clicking "Submit."

Small, consistent precautions build unbreakable protection. Share these habits with your family WhatsApp groups today!

PART 04

BATTLE AGAINST INVISIBLE DATA THIEVES

The safety of personal information faces relentless threats in our interconnected world. With data breaches now alarmingly common, millions risk having their most sensitive details exposed. This chapter examines the invisible warfare against data thieves and underscores the critical need to defend our digital identities as both a personal and collective responsibility.

4.1 Trusted Gates Crumble

I remember that uneasy feeling when I entrusted my personal details, including identity card (IC) number, home address, email ID, and phone number, to a company, only to find out that this sensitive information has been spreading online like a viral *mamak* gossip chain. This unauthorised exposure of private information is precisely what cybersecurity experts term a data breach.

A data breach occurs when unauthorised individuals gain access to confidential information, leading to potential misuse of personal or corporate data. Just like leaving my house keys under the doormat; if someone discovers them, they can enter my home without permission. Similarly, in the digital realm, if sensitive information isn't adequately protected, it becomes vulnerable to unauthorised access.

4.2 When Privacy Became a Luxury

In 2018, Malaysia grappled with a shocking privacy crisis. Over 220,000 organ donors and their families had their personal details exposed online—names, IC numbers, addresses, even phone numbers—all of which were laid bare on a public document-sharing site[16].

The leaked files dated back to 1997, and they included data from government hospitals and the National Organ Resource Centre. I recall

---

16. Malaysia faced critical data breaches involving the personal details of 220,000 organ donors, highlighting systemic vulnerabilities in data protection (Tiong, 2018).

the founder of Lowyat.net, Vijandren Ramadass, trying to get the documents taken down, but the site ignored him.

This wasn't even the first time I witnessed such negligence. Just months earlier, 46.2 million mobile users had their SIM card details, IC numbers, and addresses leaked. Foreigners living here weren't spared either. Scammers could have easily used this data to impersonate us, drain our bank accounts, or worse.

But Malaysia isn't alone. In 2017, India's Reliance Jio exposed the data of 100 million users. The world also witnessed the theft of 143 million Social Security numbers from the U.S. credit bureau Equifax. Even banks aren't immune—Bangladesh's central bank lost $81 million to hackers.

4.3 Rising Storm in Data Disasters

In December 2022, Telekom Malaysia (TM) faced a similar challenge. On December 28, they discovered that the contact information of 250,248 Unifi Mobile customers had been compromised. This breach affected both individual users and small to medium-sized enterprises (SMEs), exposing names, phone numbers, and email addresses. Fortunately, the financial details were not leaked[17].

Fast-forward to 2024, Malaysia's digital skies darkened. Our country experienced a significant surge in data breach incidents in the third quarter of 2024, with a nearly 44% increase compared to the previous quarter. This alarming trend highlights the pressing need for robust security measures to protect our personal information and maintain public trust[18].

---

[17]. *TM* addresses the data breach involving Unifi Mobile customers' contact information, December 30, 2022.

[18]. MyCERT's Q3 2024 cybersecurity report indicates a 44% quarterly surge in data breach incidents, with credential-stealing malware compromising browser-stored passwords, financial logins, and access details across 10.11% of total reported cases (December 26, 2024).

Remember: *"Storms brew in data clouds; proactive shields calm chaos."*

I've observed high-profile attacks increasingly targeting national databases, exposing sensitive personal data on a large scale. This situation underscores the importance of implementing stringent security protocols to prevent unauthorised access and data theft.

A concerning trend I've observed is that perpetrators are exfiltrating or stealing sensitive data from organisations and holding it hostage. These cybercriminals threaten to release or sell the data on the dark web unless the organisation pays a ransom within a specified timeframe. In such cases, it is crucial to report the matter to law enforcement agencies, such as the police, for assistance.

I've also noticed instances where old data breaches resurface. Perpetrators claimed to have breached data belonging to specific organisations and posted about it on the dark web. Upon my analysis, I often find that these are not new breaches but rather recycled data from incidents that occurred years ago.

These developments serve as a stark reminder of the evolving cyber threats we face. It's imperative for both organisations and individuals to stay vigilant, regularly update security measures, and foster a culture of cybersecurity awareness to safeguard our digital assets.

4.4 Massive Security Breach

As December 2024 began, Malaysia was hit with alarming news. Reports surfaced claiming that the personal data of 17 million MyKad holders had been leaked and was up for sale on the dark web. Given that Malaysia's population was projected to reach 34.1 million in 2024, this indicated that nearly half of the citizens' data might have been compromised[19].

---

[19]. This article reports on a potential leak of MyKad details in Malaysia; concerns include identity theft, untraceable cloud-based hacking, and prior breaches affecting government agencies (曾丽全, 2024).

The implications of such a massive data leak is profound. Exposure of personal information can lead to severe crimes like identity theft and financial misconduct, affecting both individuals like myself and the nation's economy.

In response to these claims, the National Registration Department (JPN) conducted internal investigations and reported no evidence of data breaches or suspicious activities within its systems. They emphasised their commitment to safeguarding citizens' data and collaborated with agencies like the National Cyber Security Agency (NACSA) and the Royal Malaysia Police for further investigations[20].

However, the evolving tactics of cybercriminals and hackers pose increasing challenges. Modern attackers often use cloud servers, making IP addresses harder to trace. This necessitates regular updates and enhancements to information security systems by both government and private entities to ensure the protection of citizens' data.

4.5 The Dark Web Déjà Vu

The vulnerabilities were exploited sooner than expected. In the January 2025 breach of Asia Recruit Malaysia—a prominent recruitment platform—hackers IntelBroker and their associates leaked sensitive user information, including identity card numbers, addresses, email addresses, and phone numbers, on the dark web. The incident raised serious concerns about data security in Malaysia[21].

The Asia Recruit Malaysia breach is part of a broader and troubling pattern of escalating cyberattacks across the country. Recent incidents have targeted critical sectors—particularly financial institutions—through malicious APK files, such as fake cleaning service apps. At

---

20. JPN denied claims of a MyKad data breach, stating no evidence was found after investigations with cybersecurity authorities and police (Bernama, 2024).

21. AnuPriya. (January 28, 2025). Massive data breach hits Asia Recruit Malaysia. CyberPress.

the same time, ransomware groups like LockBit and Hunters International have attacked businesses, compromising Active Directory servers to carry out mass encryption campaigns. Additionally, botnets, such as Avalanche-Andromeda and Ngioweb infected over 5 million IPs in Malaysia, exploiting outdated systems and enabling credential theft. The frequency and scale of these attacks highlight vulnerabilities in Malaysia's digital infrastructure, particularly in sectors relying on legacy systems (e.g., D-Link routers with unpatched CVE-2024-45698 vulnerabilities). This underscores the urgent need for enhanced cybersecurity measures, including mandatory patch management and public awareness campaigns to combat phishing and social engineering tactics[22].

In response to these challenges, the Malaysian government has introduced amendments to its Personal Data Protection Act (PDPA), mandating stricter compliance measures. These include appointing Data Protection Officers and requiring timely breach notifications to authorities. However, the persistent nature of these attacks suggests that more robust enforcement and preventive strategies are necessary to protect sensitive information effectively.

4.6 Build a Fortress Against Digital Thieves

While policy reforms are crucial, I believe the frontline defence against data thieves lies in how organisations secure their digital assets. In today's digital landscape, safeguarding company data is critical. When uploading information to the internet, it can be difficult to completely prevent unauthorised access or duplication. Even with measures like disabling "right-click copy" functions, determined individuals can still capture visible content through methods, such as photography, screenshots, or specialised extraction tools.

---

22. Data on malicious APKs, ransomware variants (LockBit, Hunters International), botnet infections (avalanche-andromeda, ngioweb), and vulnerabilities in D-Link routers (CVE-2024-45698) are sourced from CyberSecurity Malaysia's quarterly report (MyCERT, 2025).

Advancements in technology have further streamlined data acquisition. For instance, a large website comprising thousands of pages can be systematically crawled and its content downloaded in mere minutes using programming techniques, far surpassing manual copying in efficiency. This means that entire websites can be cloned during a *nasi lemak* breakfast in today's world. This reality underscores the persistent risk of data replication or leakage, whether through simple manual actions or sophisticated technical tools.

For companies, it is crucial to protect data, such as customer details, trade secrets, and other sensitive information. Implementing robust security measures is essential to mitigate the risks of data theft or leakage. One effective strategy I advocate is the deployment of tracking tools that monitor data flow within the organisation's systems. These tools can log user activities, track access to sensitive information, and detect unusual data transfers, thereby enhancing the company's ability to identify and respond to potential security breaches promptly. By maintaining comprehensive records of system interactions, companies can trace the origin of data leaks and take corrective actions to prevent future incidents.

Incorporating such monitoring solutions not only aids in safeguarding critical information but also fosters a culture of accountability and vigilance among employees, further strengthening the organisation's overall data security infrastructure.

4.7 Conclusion

In today's interconnected world, the security of personal and organisational data is not just a technical issue but a societal imperative. The rising tide of data breaches in Malaysia has far-reaching implications, affecting individual privacy, economic stability, and national security. As we navigate this digital era, it is crucial for every stakeholder—from policymakers to everyday citizens—to recognise the importance of robust data protection measures. By fostering a culture of cybersecurity awareness and implementing stringent safeguards, we can collectively build a resilient digital environment that upholds the trust and confidence of all Malaysians.

Takeaway: Cyber Shields Against Data Raiders

✓ Act Now:

- Report breaches to the police via the PDRM Cyber Crime Investigation Department (CCID) at 03-2610 1559.
- Submit screenshot proof (ransom note, dark web URL, etc.) to the MyCERT Portal within 48 hours.

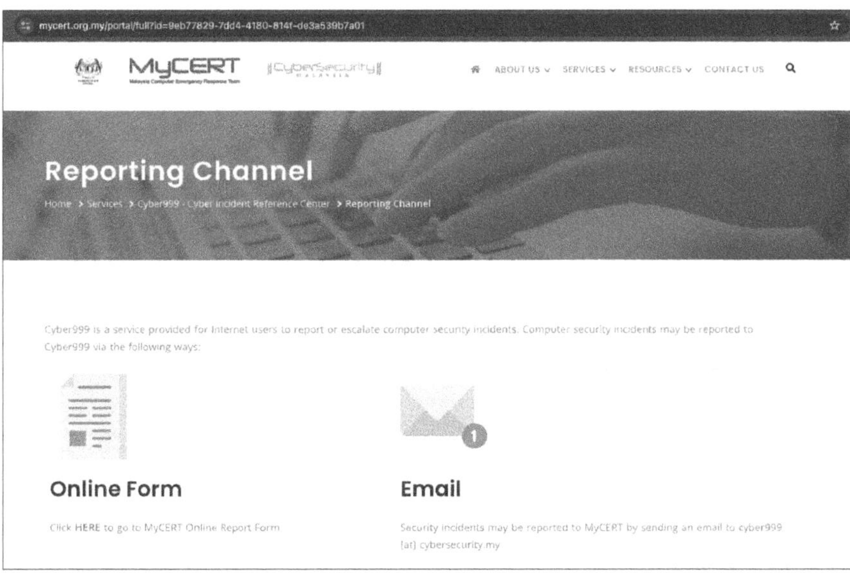

Figure 4.1 Cyber Incidents Reporting Channel in MyCERT Portal.

✖ Stop This:

- Storing IC scans in unencrypted chat apps.
- Using 'abc123' or similar weak passwords for databases.
- Ignoring software updates.

🛡 Core Defence:

- Teach data owners to password-protect personal logs.
- Run semi-annual red team exercises simulating large-scale breaches.
- Audit SME cloud security.

PART 05

WALLETS IN THE WILD

Malaysia's journey toward becoming a cashless society is reshaping daily transactions and national economic dynamics. While digital payments offer unparalleled convenience, they also demand heightened vigilance against emerging risks. Safeguarding this progress requires balancing technological adoption with robust security practices that protect both individuals and the nation's financial ecosystem.

5.1 The Evolution of Mobile Payments

Decades before I tapped my phone for *kopi kaw* payments, the e-wallet revolution began with fizzy drinks. This digital revolution was born in 1997 when Coca-Cola rigged Helsinki vending machines to accept payments via text messages [23]. Yes, you read that right! Decades before Quick Response (QR) codes, folks were buying Fanta via SMS! This quirky experiment became the world's first digital wallet, proving that even fizzy drinks could pioneer tech. Nokia soon joined the game in the mid-2000s, testing mobile payments through partnerships with banks and NFC-enabled phones[24], whose mobile payment experiments paved the way for today's e-wallets.

By the 2010s, Asia had become the epicentre of cashless transactions. In China, platforms like Alipay and WeChat Pay dominate daily life, such as buying groceries, splitting bills, and even donating to street performers. Their reach stretched beyond borders, being accepted in shops from Tokyo to Bangkok, and even right here in Malaysia. Meanwhile, global giants like Apple Pay and Google Pay quietly expanded their footprint, targeting tech-savvy urbanites from New York to Kuala Lumpur.

---

[23] In 1997, Coca-Cola introduced the world's first digital payment system through SMS-enabled vending machines in Helsinki, allowing customers to purchase beverages via text messages (Philips, 2019).

[24] Nokia advanced mobile payment technology in the mid-2000s through strategic partnerships, notably collaborating with Visa in 2008 for secure contactless transactions (Visa Inc., 2008).

5.2 The Malaysian E-Wallet Boom

An e-wallet digitises our cash and cards, allowing us to make payments with just a few taps. Today, apps like Touch 'n Go (TnG) e-wallet, GrabPay, and Boost have become household names, enabling us to pay for everything from *nasi lemak* at the local mamak stall to online shopping sprees. These e-wallets often come with perks like loyalty points, cashback offers[25], and seamless QR code payments, making transactions swift and hassle-free. Now we can even pay for our *teh tarik* by just scanning a QR code. This seamless convenience has redefined our everyday transactions across Malaysia's digital landscape.

But here in Malaysia, my love affair with e-wallets truly sparked after 2017, when giants like Touch 'n Go (TnG) teamed up with banks and telcos to launch the TnG e-wallet. Suddenly, paying for laksa at Penang hawker stalls or topping up my prepaid phone became as simple as sending a WhatsApp sticker!

5.3 From Cash to Code Payment Revolution

Malaysia made a lightning-fast leap from cash dependence to QR code dominance, sparked by the Covid-19 pandemic, accelerated by government e-wallet incentive programs, such as free RM50 sign-up bonuses, and reinforced by the convenience of avoiding the common hassle of small change. Before the pandemic, only about one in three Malaysians regularly used e-wallets. Cash was king; hawker stalls proudly displayed "*Cash Sahaja!*" signs, and uncles at wet markets scoffed at the idea of tapping phones to pay for *cendol*. But when the pandemic hit in 2020, everything changed. Fear of handling cash and lockdowns pushed even the most tech-wary uncles and aunties to embrace QR codes. By 2021, cashless payment usage skyrocketed to 79% of adults, according to Bank Negara Malaysia[26].

---

25. E-wallets like TnG, GrabPay, and Boost have become integral to daily transactions in Malaysia, offering perks, such as loyalty points and cashback (Gomes, 2022).

26. According to the World Bank's Global Findex Database 2021, as cited in *Bank Negara Malaysia*'s Annual Report (2022), 79% of adults in Malaysia used digital payments, with 42% adopting them for the first time during the pandemic.

The shift was surreal. Mamak stalls that once refused the "bank card nonsense" are now scrambling to print QR stickers, with some even offering "discount *kalau bayar guna* e-wallet!" (discount if payment is made using e-wallet). The momentum didn't stop there. By 2024, 88% of Malaysians (almost 9 in 10!) used e-wallets regularly, a significant increase from 63% in 2023. I observed that *pasar pagi* aunties now scan QR codes faster than they peel mangosteens, and cash usage in physical transactions plummeted to 36%, down from 45% just a year earlier[27].

5.4 Cashless, Not Careless

In our bustling Malaysian markets, the rise of cashless transactions brings both convenience and new challenges. Cybersecurity expert Fong Choong Fook pointed out that e-wallets currently face fewer malicious activities compared to e-banking systems; the lower risk might be due to smaller transaction limits[28]. Still, we cannot let our guard down.

Scammers are getting terrifyingly creative now. They forge QR codes at hawker stalls or clone fake e-wallet apps that closely mimic legitimate ones to trick users like us. For example, I once heard of a customer who scanned a kopitiam's QR code, saw "Payment Successful" on the phone screen with the kopitiam's name and RM50, but later realised *duit tak masuk pun* (the payment was not made). It turned out that the scammer used a fake e-wallet app that mirrored a real payment page. No money was transferred, just a sneaky way to get a free meal!

When I scan a QR code for TnG payments, I always verify the merchant's name is displayed after the scan. Legitimate businesses typically print QR codes with their official names. However, scammers can generate

---

27. Malaysia's e-wallet usage surged to 88% in 2024, driven by convenience and promotions, with cash transactions dropping to 36% as digital payments replaced physical currency (*Oppotus*, 2025).

28. Fong highlights that e-wallet security relies on device safety and lower transaction appeal for criminals, contrasting with higher-risk banking platforms (Tan, 2022).

fake QR codes in seconds and redirect payments to unauthorised accounts or malicious websites. For instance, a QR code might appear legitimate but secretly route the payment to a scammer's e-wallet instead of the intended vendor[29].

QR codes can also lead us to compromised websites. While merely visiting a deceptive site may not immediately harm our device, it could trick users, particularly elderly individuals, into downloading malicious apps. A QR code could easily redirect to a fake 'TnG update' page prompting an APK download. Once installed, such apps could hijack e-wallet credentials, track transactions, or even drain bank balances.

Remember: *"Think before you scan; scam begins with a tap."*

5.5 The Day Everything Almost Went Wrong

In late November 2023, a café owner at Seremban's Oakland New Commercial Area discovered that their payment QR code had been tampered with in an attempt to divert customer payments. Fortunately, an observant customer noticed the discrepancy in time, preventing potential losses[30].

According to news reports, the café had been operating for two months, attracting a steady stream of patrons. The owner was alerted by a vigilant customer who noticed something unusual during payment. The QR code had been overlaid with another image. Upon scanning, the payment recipient's name didn't match the café's official name, exposing the scam.

The owner expressed gratitude to the sharp-eyed customer and cautioned others to stay alert, especially during busy periods when

---

29. Scammers have exploited QR code vulnerabilities by replacing legitimate codes with their own, as seen in a case where a restaurant's TnG QR code was swapped, redirecting payments to a scammer's e-wallet. Always verify the merchant's name post-scan to avoid such risks (Oh, 2023).

30. A coffee shop in Seremban Oakland's new commercial district had its payment QR code replaced by scammers, but a vigilant customer exposed the scam, prompting businesses to enhance payment security monitoring (*Harapan Madani*, 2023).

such deceitful acts might go unnoticed. Unfortunately, the incident occurred on a hectic Sunday, and the café's CCTV system was not operational at the time, leaving the perpetrator unidentified.

This incident serves as a crucial reminder that scammers thrive in chaos. Whether it's a Sunday rush at a trendy café or lunchtime madness at my neighbourhood's *nasi lemak* stall, busy periods are prime hunting grounds for digital pickpockets and they never punch out when the crowd swells. I'm determined to remain vigilant and uncover their next move.

5.6 Cashless Transactions and the Art of Deception

At busy hawker stalls, owners often rely on customers to scan a QR code for payment while they focus on serving a long queue. In the rush, there have been incidents where customers display a payment confirmation on their phones, but the funds never reach the owner's account. Such scenarios highlight the cunning tactics some individuals employ to exploit the trust inherent in cashless transactions[31].

Unscrupulous individuals often take advantage of busy moments to deceive business operators. One prevalent method involves using old payment records or falsely claiming that a payment has been processed when it hasn't. Even though these tactics may only succeed a few times before detection, they can still result in financial losses. While some customers may be genuinely unaware due to network issues, others intentionally pretend to be unaware to avoid payment, relying on the possibility that the vendor won't double-check in the midst of the chaos. Such deceitful acts, though small in individual amounts, can accumulate to significant losses over time.

---

[31]. Malaysian vendors increasingly face e-payment scams, where perpetrators exploit busy hours to deceive businesses using outdated receipts or fake transactions (郭贞黎, 2024).

5.7 The Fake Transfer Tactic

Scammers aren't just lurking at packed hawker stalls, they're also eyeing big-ticket items. In Sungai Petani, a shopkeeper encountered a crafty individual attempting to exploit the e-wallet system. A Chinese man entered the store, showing keen interest in high-value items, and settled on an RM395 electric drill. Opting to pay via TnG eWallet, he confidently displayed a transaction record on his phone and even requested the shopkeeper to photograph the receipt. However, the cautious shopkeeper, accustomed to verifying transactions immediately, noticed that no such payment had been received. Despite the man's insistence that the transfer was complete, the shopkeeper offered to contact the TnG e-wallet customer service. Realising his ploy was unravelling, the man hastily left, promising to return later, which he never did. Upon further inspection, the shopkeeper discovered a mere one-cent transaction during that period, highlighting the scammer's exploitation of QR payments[32].

While the Sungai Petani shopkeeper escaped unscathed, shop owners in Tawau weren't so lucky. According to a news report, con artists deceived a number of shop owners by presenting fake payment receipts for high-value items. The scammers would display a convincing transaction record and request the traders to photograph the receipt, only for the traders to later discover that they'd been paid... one sen *saja*[33]!

5.8 The Parrot That Never Lies

Small businesses, such as the typical *kedai runcit*, are prime targets for such scams. Many lack robust security measures, making them easy prey for con artists. To combat this, I believe installing a sound box for

---

[32] A man allegedly scammed vendors in Kedah by editing 1-sen e-wallet transactions to mimic full payments (温丽娟, 2021).

[33] The Tawau Chinese Chamber of Commerce (CCCT) reported deceptive e-wallet transactions involving fake payment receipts for high-value purchases, leaving traders with negligible or no funds received (Toyos, 2025).

payment notifications can be an effective solution. This device gives real-time audio alerts for each transaction, announcing messages like, "Payment received, amount eight ringgit," much like having a loyal parrot squawking, "*Dah dapat duit, boss!*" This functionality allows merchants like me to immediately verify successful payments. These sound boxes can also connect to smartphones, enabling me to cross-check transaction details, such as the amount, time, and payment status.

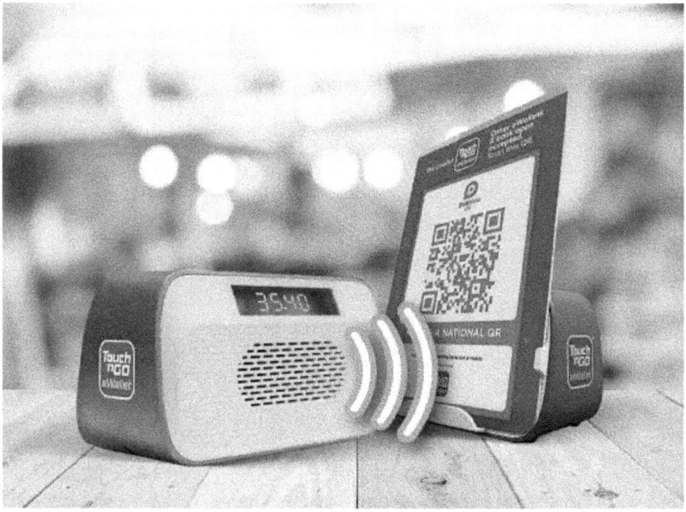

Figure 5.1 A Touch 'n Go e-wallet soundbox.

Solely relying on a customer's displayed "payment successful" screen is insufficient; merchants need dependable verification methods to safeguard their interests. The dual verification (combining audio alerts with mobile app confirmations) significantly enhances transaction security and helps prevent scammers from using fake payment interfaces to deceive merchants.

It is critical for small businesses to implement these measures to prevent increasingly sophisticated scams in the digital payments space.

5.9 Conclusion

In today's rapidly evolving digital landscape, Malaysia stands at the forefront of the e-wallet revolution. As we embrace this shift towards cashless transactions, it's imperative that we remain vigilant against emerging digital scams that threaten our financial security. The widespread adoption of e-wallets has undeniably transformed the way Malaysians conduct daily transactions, offering unparalleled convenience and efficiency. However, this digital shift also necessitates a heightened awareness of potential security threats. By staying informed and adopting proactive measures, we can collectively safeguard our financial well-being in this digital era.

Takeaway: Double-check before Accepting Payment

✓ Act Now:

- Install sound boxes for payment notifications at your payment counter.
- Cross-check transactions via e-wallet merchant apps before handing over high-value items.
- Assist uncles and aunties to recognise fake e-wallet interfaces.

✖ Stop This:

- Trusting customers' "payment successful" screens without app confirmation.
- Using generic QR codes without your shop name embedded or displayed.
- Leaving sound boxes on mute during rush hours.

🛡 Core Defence:

- Adopt a dual-layer verification:
    - Sound boxes with tri-lingual announcements.
    - Sound box connects to the smartphone to sync transaction details.

PART 06

DIGITAL IMPERSONATION AND ITS VICTIMS

As Malaysia accelerates its digital transformation, cybercriminals exploit vulnerabilities through increasingly sophisticated tactics. Phishing, domain spoofing, and digital impersonation now threaten not just individual security but national stability. Combating these risks demands collaboration across all sectors (from citizens to policymakers) to fortify defences and foster a resilient digital society.

6.1 Mechanics of Domain and Subdomain Abuse

A long time ago, I encountered a scam where someone purchased a domain and altered it to mimic RHB, a bank I used. I received an email disguised as an official RHB notification, which included a deceptive link labelled "Secure Login Portal" urging me to "verify my account" for account protection. When I clicked the link and tried to log in, my password kept getting rejected. Upon closer inspection, I realised the URL was fake. For example, if the legitimate website is *rhbbank.com*, a scammer could create a subdomain like *rhb.commercialbank1.com* and embed it in phishing emails. Unfamiliar users, misled by the email's urgency, might assume the link is legitimate, enter their credentials, and unknowingly hand over their username and password to hackers.

Remember: *"Read the full link—think before you click."*

Figure 6.1 Example of a fake RHB URL.

Figure 6.2 Example of a fake Maybank URL.

To understand how such scams work, it is essential to clarify the concepts of domains and subdomains. A domain is a primary web address (e.g., *primeholdings.com*). A subdomain is a prefix added to the main domain (e.g., *maybank.primeholdings.com*). Scammers often register fictitious but credible-sounding domains or create subdomains to impersonate trusted brands. For instance, if a scammer registers primeholdings.com and designs a subdomain like maybank.primeholdings.com, they can replicate Maybank's official login page. Unsuspecting users might enter their credentials, believing the site to be legitimate. Cloned websites and applications can appear identical to genuine ones, making the use of fake subdomains a potent phishing tactic. This allows attackers to syphon funds directly from victims' bank accounts, often before the breach is detected.

6.2 When Technical Deception Meets Human Trust

These technical foundations set the stage for more insidious threats. Based on domain spoofing, phishing weaponises this deception to exploit human psychology. Specifically, phishing is a cyberattack method where attackers impersonate legitimate entities to deceive victims into revealing sensitive information, such as login credentials or financial details. Its effectiveness hinges on manipulating domain and subdomain structures to create counterfeit websites indistinguishable from genuine ones.

The term itself comes from an analogy to 'fishing.' While fishing casts a line to catch fish, phishing sends deceptive messages to hook humans, exploiting trust instead of bait. For example, a scammer might register *public-bank-update.com* or abuse a subdomain like *security.public.bank.net* to host a cloned login page. Users, unaware of how website addresses are structured, often overlook subtle discrepancies and submit their credentials, enabling attackers to hijack accounts. Ultimately, this synergy of technical deception (domain spoofing) and psychological manipulation (urgency-driven prompts) defines modern phishing campaigns.

6.3 Early Instances of Domain Spoofing

These tactics are not new. Globally, as early as 2003, attackers had begun exploiting domain spoofing, mimicking legitimate commerce sites like eBay and PayPal, using subtle variations, such as ebay-update.com or paypal-security.net to exploit inattentive users. These domains hosted spoofed pages that mirrored authentic interfaces, while email worm programs mass-distributed phishing emails directing recipients to these fake sites. Under the guise of "updating account security," victims were prompted to enter passwords, credit card details, and other sensitive information[34]. This era cemented domain spoofing as a core phishing technique, demonstrating how cybercriminals weaponise URL similarities to bypass user vigilance and institutional safeguards.

Malaysia was not immune to this. By February 2004, local banks faced similar phishing campaigns exploiting domain deception. RHB Bank customers received deceptive emails urging them to "validate" accounts via a link to *rhbbank.com.my* (RHB's legitimate domain at the time). However, embedded within the email was a malicious IP address (*210.192.42.34/img/in.htm*) redirecting users to a counterfeit RHB Bank login page hosted in Taiwan. MyCERT, Malaysia's national cybersecurity agency, confirmed the attack after verifying with RHB Bank that no such emails were authorised[35].

Later that year in September, another high-profile phishing campaign targeted Citibank customers in Malaysia. MyCERT issued an advisory detailing deceptive emails impersonating Citibank, which directed recipients to a spoofed login page via a malicious link. Unlike the earlier RHB Bank attack that exploited IP addresses, this campaign used deceptive URLs (e.g., *https://secure.citibank.com* or *https://login.citibank-*

---

[34] In late 2003, phishers registered deceptive domains mimicking legitimate sites, using email worms to distribute spoofed messages that redirected users to spoofed pages under the guise of "account updates" (Phishing.org, n.d.).

[35] In February 2004, MyCERT reported a phishing incident involving emails impersonating RHB Bank, which directed users to a counterfeit website designed to steal internet banking credentials (MyCERT, 2004).

update.net) to mimic Citibank's legitimate banking portal. By appending legitimate-sounding subdomains (e.g., "secure" or "login") to deceptive domains, attackers created URLs that appeared official to unsuspecting users. Victims were prompted to enter their usernames and passwords under false pretences, enabling attackers to hijack these accounts for financial theft. MyCERT confirmed that Citibank did not authorise these communications[36], emphasising the attackers' use of urgency-driven social engineering and visually cloned interfaces. Attackers aimed to harvest Internet banking credentials through these spoofed pages, mirroring global patterns of using deceptive domains and urgency-driven messaging to steal financial data.

6.4 Phishing's Platform Evolution

Two decades later, the same deception persists, only the platforms have changed. Despite decades of advancements in cybersecurity, Malaysians continue to fall victim to phishing tactics that remain fundamentally unchanged, though their delivery channels have evolved. First, in 2023, John (a pseudonym) received an email mimicking his bank's official communication, urging "urgent account verification" via a link to a cloned banking portal. Believing the domain (*secure-banklogin.com*) to be legitimate, he entered his credentials and one-time password (OTP), only to lose thousands of ringgit within minutes. By the time John realised the scam, funds had been laundered through layered transactions, making recovery impossible[37]. His story mirrors countless others, where attackers persistently exploit human trust in familiar domains, even as banks enhance email filters and SMS alerts.

---

36. In September 2004, MyCERT identified a phishing scam where emails impersonating Citibank directed recipients to a counterfeit website to steal their online banking credentials (MyCERT, 2004).

37. In 2023, a Malaysian bank customer, John (a pseudonym), fell victim to a phishing attack after receiving a spoofed email mimicking his bank's official communication. The email tricked him into "verifying his account" via a malicious link. Trusting its legitimacy, he entered his login credentials and OTP, resulting in an immediate loss of thousands of ringgit and underscoring the persistent risk of domain spoofing (Wahab & Hisham, 2025).

John's 2023 ordeal foreshadowed a persistent threat. Even in 2025, this tried-and-tested scam formula persists. Only now, attackers have expanded their reach beyond emails to dominate mainstream and emerging platforms. Although heightened public awareness and improved banking safeguards occur regularly, cybercriminals in Malaysia continue to exploit domain spoofing techniques, adapting their methods to mainstream social media like Facebook while branching out to newer channels like WhatsApp and TikTok. A 2025 phishing campaign impersonating Bank Islam exemplifies this trend. Bank Islam Malaysia alerted the public to deceptive Facebook posts claiming the bank was conducting a "loyalty lottery" with prizes worth millions. These posts misused the bank's name and imagery, directing users to a counterfeit website mimicking *bankislam.com.my*. These pages harvested victims' online banking credentials under the guise of prize registration. The scammers even repurposed photos from a legitimate event held by the bank in September 2023, where prizes were awarded to investment account holders[38]. This case mirrors earlier tactics of subdomain spoofing but leverages social media's viral reach for wider impact.

From cloned portals to viral posts, the core deception remains. This scam underscores a persistent truth in which attackers adapt their delivery channels while retaining core technical strategies like domain spoofing. As banks fortified email filters and SMS authentication, modern scammers have expanded their reach to social media platforms like Facebook, exploiting user trust in familiar brands and the rapid spread of social content.

6.5 Essential Defences Against Web Spoofing

To counter these evolving threats, proactive measures are essential. When visiting a website, I would avoid immediately logging in. First, I verify that

---

[38] In February 2025, Bank Islam Malaysia and Malaysian police alerted the public to deceptive Facebook posts falsely claiming the bank was conducting an online lottery with substantial prizes (Mamat, 2025).

the URL matches the legitimate domain. If I accidentally enter my username or password on a suspicious site, I immediately contact my bank or service provider to report the incident and request account security checks.

When encountering suspicious websites, I verify their authenticity using tools like MYNIC | WHOIS (*https://mynic.my/whois*) to check the domain's creation date. If a domain was registered very recently (e.g., in 2025 or a few months prior), it may be a scam. Legitimate websites often have longer operational histories, as scams are typically reported and shut down quickly. A long-standing domain with no history of complaints is statistically less likely to be malicious. I always cross-check URLs before entering sensitive information and remain vigilant for subtle typos or unusual subdomains in web addresses. I educate myself about URL structures to recognise discrepancies between legitimate domains and impersonated subdomains.

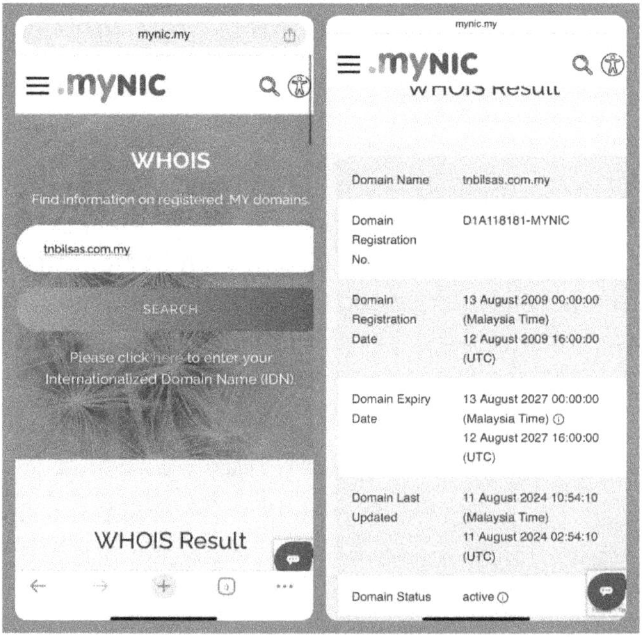

Figure 6.3 Using MYNIC | WHOIS to verify domain registration records.

The following is a list of local and foreign banks operating in Malaysia, along with their respective websites, accurate as of 21 May 2025.

Bank Name	Website
Affin Bank Berhad	https://www.affinbank.com.my
Alliance Bank Malaysia Berhad	https://www.alliancebank.com.my
AmBank (M) Berhad	https://www.ambank.com.my
Bangkok Bank Berhad	https://www.bangkokbank.com.my
Bank of America Malaysia Berhad	https://www.bankofamerica.com
Bank of China (Malaysia) Berhad	https://www.bankofchina.com.my
MUFG Bank (Malaysia) Berhad	https://www.bk.mufg.jp/malaysia
CIMB Bank Berhad	https://www.cimb.com
Citibank Berhad	https://www.citibank.com.my
Deutsche Bank (Malaysia) Berhad	https://www.db.com/malaysia
Hong Leong Bank Berhad	https://www.hlb.com.my
HSBC Bank Malaysia Berhad	https://www.hsbc.com.my
Industrial and Commercial Bank of China (Malaysia) Berhad	https://www.icbcmy.com
J.P. Morgan Chase Bank Berhad	https://www.jpmorgan.com/global/my
Malayan Banking Berhad (Maybank)	https://www.maybank2u.com.my
OCBC Bank (Malaysia) Berhad	https://www.ocbc.com.my
Public Bank Berhad	https://www.publicbank.com.my
RHB Bank Berhad	https://www.rhbgroup.com
Standard Chartered Bank Malaysia Berhad	https://www.sc.com/my
Sumitomo Mitsui Banking Corporation Malaysia Berhad	https://www.smbc.co.jp/global/malaysia
The Bank of Nova Scotia Berhad	https://www.scotiabank.com/en/global/malaysia.html
United Overseas Bank (Malaysia) Bhd.	https://www.uob.com.my

Table 6.1 The list of banks operating in Malaysia.

For a comprehensive list of banks, you can refer to Bank Negara Malaysia's list of regulated entities.

6.6 Conclusion

Digital impersonation is a challenge that we all must take seriously. It's not just about protecting our information; it's about contributing to a safer online environment for everyone in Malaysia. By staying alert and taking simple actions to verify websites and emails, we can collectively reduce the risk of falling victim to these scams. As a nation, we must work together to raise awareness and share knowledge about these threats. The stronger our collective vigilance, the safer our digital world will be.

Takeaway: Steady Vigilance for a Secure Digital Identity

✓ Act Now:

- Always type a bank URL manually in the browser and remember to bookmark it.
- Double-check the URL domain details for subtle errors, such as extra characters, unusual subdomains, or minor spelling errors.
- Check the registration date and legitimacy of suspicious domains by using validation tools, such as MYNIC | WHOIS or similar services.

✖ Stop This:

- Immediate clicks on the emails or pop-ups that claim to be about urgent security updates.
- Logging in through the links in emails or messages that mimic familiar brands but appear suspicious.

Core Defence:

- The real way to prevent digital impersonation lies in a combination of layered approaches:
    - Technical checks like URL inspection and domain verification.
    - A healthy dose of scepticism.

PART 07

EMAIL THREATS IN CORPORATE ENVIRONMENTS

Email remains a cornerstone of modern communication, yet its ubiquity makes it a prime target for cyberattacks. Businesses and individuals alike face growing threats ranging from phishing scams to malware-laden attachments. Strengthening email security is no longer optional but a necessity to preserve trust and operational integrity in Malaysia's evolving digital landscape.

7.1 The Evolution of Communication

From ancient carrier pigeons to the invention of postal systems and eventually digital communication, I have always marvelled at how the evolution of messaging has been pivotal to human collaboration. Unlike the physical delays of traditional mail or the need for immediate interaction during phone calls, I experienced the revolutionary impact of email. It is a medium that is asynchronous, instant, and recordable, which completely transformed how I operate in the business world.

This revolutionary tool, now fundamental to global commerce, began as a modest experiment in digital connectivity. I was fascinated to discover that the origins of email date back to 1971, when Ray Tomlinson, a computer engineer at Bolt, Beranek and Newman (BBN), conducted an experiment to test data exchange between two computers. He sent the first email containing the text "QWERTYUIOP"[39], and this breakthrough not only demonstrated that machines could communicate seamlessly but also laid the groundwork for what has become an indispensable tool in my modern business operations.

From its humble beginnings, email rapidly evolved into a multifaceted tool that reshaped corporate workflows through its core strengths. Many benefitted from its capability to transmit information globally within seconds, archive conversations, slash communication costs, and enable multitasking. This technology revolutionised my digital correspondence,

---

[39]. The first email, containing the text "QWERTYUIOP," was sent by Ray Tomlinson as part of an experiment between two computers at BNN (*Guinness World Records*, n.d.).

boosting my efficiency by allowing me to manage invoices, negotiate contracts, and prioritise urgent tasks without requiring simultaneous participation. I appreciate how its cost-effectiveness and instant collaboration across time zones has allowed me, for instance, to finalise a contract with London partners overnight, bypassing the time zone barriers that would otherwise hinder phone-based coordination.

Yet, I am also aware that the very features that empower businesses (speed, accessibility, and global reach) create avenues for exploitation. As email became a lifeline for my business operations, I learnt that attackers began exploiting its widespread reliance, transforming what was once a tool of progress into a conduit for phishing and spoofing attacks.

Remember: *"Convenience opens doors, vigilance keeps them shut."*

In my corporate environment, I use email platforms like Microsoft Outlook and Google Gmail, which are the prime targets for attackers. Given that these are the world's most widely used email services,[40] I understand why attackers prioritise these platforms to maximise potential victims due to their massive user bases. This vast reach allows them to distribute malicious content at scale, with deceptive emails becoming their weapon of choice. I remain cautious of suspicious emails with unclear origins or attachments. These emails often impersonate trusted entities or colleagues and use emotionally manipulative language to lure me into clicking malicious links or attachments. I am fully aware that clicking on these embedded files may trigger unauthorised installations on my device, often without my knowledge. These actions can lead to severe consequences, which attackers typically categorise into two types of attacks, which include disruptive malware that cripples internal systems and sophisticated financial scams exploiting offshore entities.

---

[40]. Google and Microsoft account for 7% and 6% respectively of global branded phishing attempts (*Smith*, 2024).

7.2 Malware Attacks and Operational Disruption

Malware-driven attacks stand out for their dual capacity to cripple operations and inflict lasting reputational damage. By seizing control of email accounts, attackers achieve two goals: first, they amplify their reach by spamming the victim's contacts; second, they paralyse the victim's ability to operate, forcing individuals or organisations into costly system overhauls.

Once installed, the malware may exploit a compromised account to send thousands of deceptive emails (from phishing links to malware-laden attachments) to every contact in one's address book. These mass-sending strategies serve multiple purposes, which include infecting more devices, harvesting sensitive data, and creating chaos to divert attention from other malicious activities.

Such methods are not new. The 2000 ILOVEYOU worm, for example, spread via a malicious email attachment disguised as a love letter, tricking users like myself into opening "LOVE-LETTER-FOR-YOU.txt. vbs" under the illusion of a harmless text file[41]. The worm's success lay in its ability to exploit human curiosity and trust, and this is a psychological lever that attackers still use today.

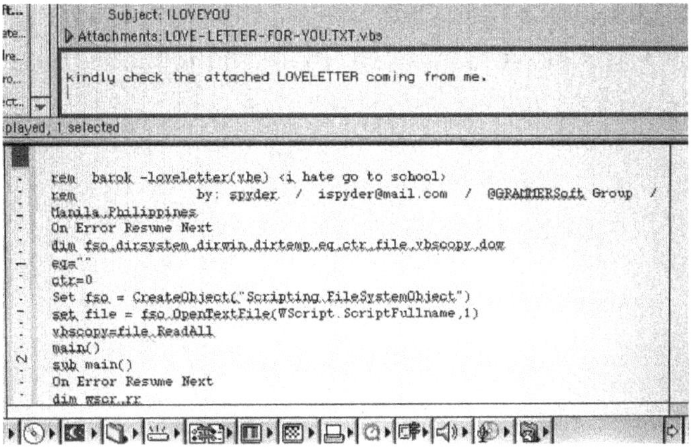

Figure 7.1 The ILOVEYOU virus pandemic in 2000.

---

41. The ILOVEYOU worm, distributed in May 2000, used a Visual Basic script (.vbs) disguised as a text file (Winder, 2020).

This type of attack not only overwhelms an email server's capacity—triggering automatic security lockdowns or blacklisting by service providers, as occurred when the Pentagon and U.K. Parliament shut down their email systems during the ILOVEYOU outbreak—but also damages the victim's professional reputation. Such attacks can corrupt critical system files or consume excessive memory resources. The ILOVEYOU worm overwrote random files (from documents to photographs) while self-replicating across networks without requiring user interaction, infecting 50 million Windows computers within 10 days and causing an estimated $10 billion in recovery costs. It can cause email clients to freeze, crash repeatedly, or permanently lose access to synced data. As a result, the email service becomes unusable. In such cases, the only remedy is often a full system reformat to purge the infection, which in turn causes significant downtime and data loss. Attackers capitalise on this desperation, aware that some companies may pay the ransom to avoid irreversible losses.

7.3 Phishing-Driven Financial Exploitation

Beyond overt system disruption, I have witnessed more sophisticated and stealthier tactics. For instance, spyware installed on compromised devices can scan my communications and financial records, enabling attackers to weaponise stolen data to craft highly targeted phishing emails. I have seen cases where attackers impersonate the victim (in this case, me) and send deceptive payment requests to my clients or suppliers. These emails may mimic my company's tone and branding, thereby increasing their credibility. To further deceive recipients, attackers may spoof domain names (e.g., *maybank.corporation.com*) or replicate official email templates. These technical deceptions are merely the first layer of Business Email Compromise (BEC) attacks. To maximise success rates, attackers frequently enhance authenticity by hijacking legitimate email accounts or inserting deceptive requests into ongoing email threads, as was seen in the 2013-2015 Quanta

Computer scam, where USD 121 million was syphoned from Facebook and Google through altered invoices[42]. Although the attackers have been arrested and both companies have recovered their losses in that instance, such success stories are rare. BEC scams often result in irreparable financial losses. This is a harsh reality currently facing businesses around the world, including those in Malaysia.

Closer to home, Malaysian businesses, like the logistics company in Batu Pahat, are now being targeted by similar scams. In April 2024, the company suffered losses totalling RM321,698.74 after a cashier transferred funds to an overseas bank account. The attacker impersonated a foreign business partner via email, notifying of a new account change and requesting a payment of RM448,215.11 for container rental costs. I can imagine the distress when, without verifying the change, the victim transferred funds to the designated account on April 2, only to later learn upon contacting the actual company representative that no such email had been sent. According to Batu Pahat police, the deceptive email closely mimicked the partner's legitimate address, which is a hallmark of BEC scams. Despite notifying the bank to cancel the money transfer, only RM122,709.76 was returned to the company's account[43]. This is a stark reminder that BEC's borderless nature underscores the need for universal vigilance.

Such exploitation thrives by manipulating the trust inherent in routine operations to deceive employees while exposing vulnerabilities that lie beyond the reach of traditional cybersecurity tools (e.g., firewalls, antivirus software, and intrusion detection systems designed to block malware, not human manipulation). Unwary recipients, especially

---

42. Between 2013 and 2015, attackers orchestrated a BEC scam by impersonating Quanta Computer, a legitimate hardware supplier, and altering invoices to deceive Google and Facebook into transferring approximately $23 million and $98 million, respectively (IBM, 2023).

43. In April 2024, a Batu Pahat logistics company lost RM321,698.74 to a BEC scam after transferring funds to an overseas bank account following a spoofed email requesting payment of RM448,215.11 for container rental costs, with partial recovery efforts reclaiming RM122,709.76 (Shadiqe, 2024).

those unfamiliar with cybersecurity red flags, may comply with these requests, leading to substantial financial losses.

7.4 Offshore Deception via Legal Loopholes

Parallel to direct email hijacking, offshore registration loopholes provide attackers with a veneer of legitimacy to syphon funds undetected. Certain jurisdictions permit the registration of nearly identical company names to those of legitimate businesses. For example, a Malaysian company named "OPERiON Ecommerce Sdn Bhd" could be replicated as "OPERiON Ecommerce Offshore Sdn Bhd" in an offshore territory like the British Virgin Islands. Scammers then open bank accounts under these cloned entities, enabling them to receive unauthorised payments while evading detection through jurisdictional complexity.

In addition to offshore scams, direct email account hijacking poses equal risks. In March 2016, Shanghai's Anti-Telecom Network Scam Centre thwarted a €2.99 million BEC attack targeting a multinational company. Cybercriminals had breached the company's email system, impersonated its CEO, and directed a deceptive wire transfer to an offshore Agricultural Bank of China account. I was impressed by how authorities froze the account within 30 minutes and arrested three suspects attempting to withdraw the funds[44], which is a testament to both the sophistication of these scams and the critical need for rapid response.

While I recognise that specific offshore locations are not named here, I always verify the legitimacy of any entity requesting fund transfers, especially those claiming ties to offshore operations.

---

44. On March 31, 2016, Shanghai's Anti-Telecom Fraud Centre intercepted a €2.99 million BEC scam. Cybercriminals impersonated a CEO via compromised email, directing a deceptive transfer to an offshore account. Authorities froze the funds within 30 minutes and arrested three suspects attempting withdrawals (People's Daily, 2016).

7.5 Proactive Prevention, Rapid Response

I firmly believe that, while these threats are formidable, my company and I can mitigate risks through systematic prevention and decisive incident management. I have implemented mandatory cybersecurity training for all employees, emphasising email verification protocols, such as confirming payment requests via secondary channels, like phone calls. I also rely on advanced email filtering tools to flag suspicious domains, mismatched sender addresses, or unusual language patterns. I enforce strict financial controls, such as multi-level approval processes for high-value transactions and regular audits of vendor databases. Additionally, I have cultivated a culture of scepticism by encouraging employees to report anomalies immediately, and I participate in routine simulated phishing exercises to reinforce our collective vigilance.

If a scam occurs, acting swiftly is crucial to minimising damage. I immediately contacted the bank to freeze affected accounts and attempt transaction reversals. I ensure that all digital evidence, including email headers, attachments, and transaction records, is preserved for forensic analysis. I notify our internal IT teams to isolate compromised systems, reset credentials, and scan for malware. Simultaneously, I file a report with local law enforcement and cybersecurity agencies, such as Malaysia's National Cyber Security Agency (NACSA), and I make sure to publicly warn partners and clients to prevent secondary exploitation of stolen data.

While corporate email scams exploit both technological vulnerabilities and human trust, their impact can be mitigated through proactive education, robust safeguards, and rapid response protocols. As attackers continually refine their tactics, I prioritise adaptive defences, cross-departmental collaboration, and transparency in incident reporting. By fostering a security-first mindset, I have transformed email from a potential liability into a secure pillar of modern operations.

7.6 Conclusion

This chapter not only emphasises the importance of cybersecurity in the workplace but also highlights the broader societal implications of email threats. As a nation that continues to grow in digital capacity, Malaysia must stay ahead of cyber threats by fostering a culture of awareness and taking decisive actions to protect personal and corporate data.

Takeaway: Email Security, Corporate Priority

✓ Act Now:

- Always verify the sender address of every email and double-check domain details before clicking a link or opening an attachment.
- Use powerful email advanced filters and multi-factor authentication.

✖ Stop This:

- Taking quick action to respond to urgent payment or account change requests without verification.
- Ignoring internal approval processes or skip security training updates.

🛡 Core Defence:

- Continuous vigilance and strict adherence to verification processes.
- Regular employee training and layered technical defences.

PART 08

SECURING SECOND-HAND PHONE

The booming second-hand mobile market offers affordability but hides risks ranging from stolen devices to tampered hardware. Consumers often unknowingly purchase compromised phones, facing financial losses and privacy breaches. Raising awareness and promoting ethical practices are vital steps to protect Malaysians in this unregulated yet pervasive marketplace.

8.1 The Role of Factory Resets

In my experience, keeping up with the latest technology can be expensive. That's why I've often turned to buying preowned mobile phones, especially when I'm watching my budget or trying to embrace sustainability. Here in Malaysia, second-hand phones have grown in popularity as a cost-effective alternative to new devices. However, I've learnt that a second-hand phone isn't simply a "used phone" in the traditional sense. Because the inner workings of a device may have been altered by previous owners, I now always assume that the phone may not be in a "clean" state. In fact, many experts advise that a preowned phone should be treated as if it needs a full factory reset, which means restoring it completely to its original settings before I start using it.

The reason is simple: because I have no way of knowing what kind of software or hidden applications might still be lurking inside a used device. I worry about programs that could monitor my phone's location, read my text messages, record my calls, access my contacts, or even activate my camera and microphone without my knowledge. I can't risk having my address book or messaging history exposed, or worse, an app secretly spying on me. That's why I always insist on a complete factory reset before I put a preowned phone to work.

Figure 8.1 Example of Factory Reset for iPhone

8.2 Understanding Second-hand Phones

When I talk about a preowned phone, I'm referring to a device that has been used before, but I've come to understand that within the electronics world there are different categories: phones that are bought and sold by reputable retailers; certified refurbished models from original manufacturers; and devices sold privately by individuals[45]. Each category has its own risks and benefits.

I find preowned devices attractive because they offer a way for me to experience high-end technology at a fraction of the cost of a new phone.

---

45. For definitions of "used," "refurbished," and "Certified Pre-Owned" devices and their associated risks, see *Verizon* (2023).

For example, I might be able to buy a flagship device that once retailed at a very high price only to find a second-hand version at a considerably lower price. Additionally, buying a used phone appeals to my environmental values since reusing a device helps reduce electronic waste and supports a more sustainable lifestyle.

In Malaysia, the market for preowned phones is growing rapidly[46]. I often explore various online marketplaces, local retailers, and even official stores that offer certified refurbished phones. When I purchase from these trusted outlets, I gain the assurance that the device has undergone quality testing and has been reset to its original state. However, I'm also aware that not all used devices come from reputable sources. Some sellers, especially on less-regulated platforms, may not take the necessary steps to ensure that the device is free of unwanted software or hidden applications.

This is where the concept of a "full factory reset" becomes absolutely crucial. I always assume that the device might contain software that can track my activities, so I make it a point to reset the phone completely, as if I were starting with a brand-new device. Some software on used devices may have the ability to monitor my GPS location, read my messages, listen in on calls, and even view my contacts or photos. I have read discussions online about how certain applications can silently activate the camera or microphone without my consent. The simple fact for me is that if a used phone isn't properly reset, I'm potentially giving up access to sensitive personal data.

Imagine a scenario where I buy a second-hand phone without performing a reset. If the device still has preinstalled applications from the previous owner, those apps could be designed to send data to an external server. They might log every keystroke, capture images, or record conversations.

---

[46]. Malaysia's used smartphone market grew at a 12.8% CAGR from 2016–2021 and is projected to expand further at 14.9% through 2026F, driven by 5G adoption, government digitalisation efforts, and rising new phone prices (Banerjee, 2022).

Even though these risks might seem extreme, I've seen reports from mobile security experts describing cases where seemingly innocuous apps were used for such purposes. For me, and many Malaysians who buy from various sources, this risk is not negligible. That's why I always verify that a used device has been thoroughly reset before I use it.

If a seller claims the phone has been "wiped," there is no guarantee that all remnants of previous data have been completely removed. Given that modern smartphones have complex storage systems, sometimes a simple erase isn't enough to clear out all hidden files or applications. That's why my best practice is to perform a full factory reset myself once I purchase the device. By doing so, I ensure that the operating system is installed fresh and that any malicious software that might have been added is removed.

In summary, a second-hand phone can be an excellent choice if I am careful about where I buy it from and if I take the time to secure it. Understanding the nature of preowned devices and the importance of starting with a clean slate is the first step in protecting my privacy.

8.3 The Hidden Dangers

The appeal of a second-hand phone lies in its affordability and the opportunity to get a high-quality device without paying full price. Yet, this benefit can come at a hidden cost, namely security and privacy risks. I must consider the possibility that the device has not been completely cleared of its past; unwanted software might still be installed, capable of tracking various aspects of my digital life[47].

One of my biggest concerns is that some preowned phones may have software that can track my phone's GPS. This means someone else could monitor my movements without my permission. In today's digital

---

47. While modern Android phones use file-based encryption and AES-256 standards to protect data post-factory reset, advanced forensic tools (e.g., Cellebrite) can theoretically bypass encryption (Bhutani, 2023).

age, my location data is incredibly sensitive. Whether I'm at home, at work, or travelling, my whereabouts can reveal a lot about my habits and routines, and I find it very disturbing.

I also worry that hidden programs could access my messages and voice calls. I can't imagine every text or conversation being available for someone else to read or listen to. If I use messaging applications like WeChat or Telegram on a second-hand phone, I might be exposing myself to significant risks. It's not just about losing my privacy; it's about compromising personal relationships, professional communications, and even financial information that I might share via secure messaging platforms.

For me, the risk extends even further. A used phone might have hidden software that can send my entire contact list to an external server, potentially exposing not only my contacts but also those of my friends, family, and business associates. The thought of such data being exploited for identity theft or targeted marketing is alarming.

Moreover, I'm cautious about reports suggesting that certain applications can remotely activate a phone's camera or microphone[48]. The idea that my phone could be used to record my surroundings without my consent is not just a privacy breach; it's a serious security threat. With this in mind, I always insist on performing a full factory reset on any preowned phone I purchase.

The notion of a second-hand phone being "as new" is misleading if the device is not properly reset. The previous owner may have installed tracking software or other covert applications. These apps might not even show up in my regular app list, and only a full factory reset can remove these risks entirely. It is for this reason that the advice to treat every second-hand phone as a full factory reset is so important.

---

[48]. Preowned smartphones may contain spyware enabling remote activation of cameras/ microphones (Chmura, Hansen, Hargrove, & Jackson, 2019).

If I purchase a used phone without resetting it completely, I might unknowingly allow someone to track my movements, listen to my conversations, or see my personal messages. The potential for abuse in such a scenario is immense.

These risks are not just theoretical. Mobile security experts have documented instances where second-hand devices contained persistent software capable of tracking user activity long after the device was sold. Sometimes, the previous owner might not have even been aware of the software installed on the phone, while in other cases, a malicious seller might intentionally leave the software in place to profit from reselling the data.

Furthermore, if I don't fully reset the phone, remnants of my previous owner's data might remain. Depending on how the phone manages its storage, it is sometimes possible to recover such leftover data, even after an apparent wipe. For someone with malicious intent, recovering deleted data could reveal personal information, financial details, or even passwords that could compromise my accounts.

The bottom line for me is that the dangers hidden in a used phone are real, and they can affect various aspects of my personal and professional life. Whether it is my location, my communications, or my personal contacts, every bit of data stored on a device can be a potential target for exploitation if not properly cleared.

8.4 Steps to Perform a Secure Wipe

One of the most critical steps to take when purchasing a second-hand phone is to perform a full factory reset. This procedure restores the device to the state it was in when it originally left the factory, wiping away all previous data and software modifications. For me, the idea of a factory reset might seem like a technical detail, but I consider it the single most effective method of ensuring that any potentially harmful software is removed.

Whenever I purchase a second-hand phone, one of the most critical steps for me is to perform a full factory reset. This process is essential because it restores the device to the condition it was in when it originally left the manufacturing plant, wiping away all previous data and software modifications. Even if a seller claims that the phone has been "wiped," I never take their word for it; I will perform the reset myself. Merely deleting files or formatting the storage isn't enough since data remnants can sometimes be recovered. That's why I make sure to reinstall the entire operating system through a full factory reset. This way, I eliminate any covert applications, malicious programs, or residual user data that might compromise my privacy[49].

A used phone might contain an application that tracks my movements, messages, or calls; if I do not perform a factory reset, that application could remain hidden on my device, silently gathering information every time I use it. On the other hand, when I take the time to reset the phone fully, I'm starting with a clean slate. I feel secure when the operating system is freshly installed, with no old apps or data remaining to compromise my privacy.

The reset process is straightforward on most modern smartphones. I typically navigate to the settings menu, find the system options, and select the reset function. Once I confirm my decision, the phone reboots and wipes all stored data. Even though the exact steps may vary depending on the make and model, the underlying principle remains the same, which is I completely remove all traces of previous use, ensuring that I start with a clean slate[50].

However, just deleting files or formatting the storage is not sufficient. Often, the right tools can recover data remnants. That's why I always

---

49. A factory reset is critical for preowned devices as it reinstalls the operating system and erases residual data or malware, ensuring a secure baseline (Culbert, 2021).

50. A factory reset, while varying in steps between iOS and Android devices (e.g., account removal, FRP deactivation), universally ensures complete data erasure and OS reinstallation to eliminate residual user traces (Hill, 2024).

perform a full factory reset, involving reinstalling the entire operating system. This is a far more effective method than a mere delete or quick format. Whenever I buy a used phone, I always stress the point of starting from scratch.

The message is clear here in Malaysia, where many people buy second-hand devices from local shops or online platforms. I never trust a device just because the seller claims it has undergone cleaning. I always perform the reset myself once I have the phone in hand. This small step, I believe, can save me from a world of trouble later on.

There are additional benefits that come from a full factory reset. It enables me to customise the device precisely to my liking, establishing my security features from the beginning, including biometric locks, strong passwords, and two-factor authentication. By customising the settings myself, I ensure that no unwanted programs or configurations carried over from a previous owner are left behind.

Moreover, starting fresh with a reset device helps me avoid potential issues with outdated software. Occasionally, an older operating system on a phone may no longer receive security updates. By resetting and then updating the device to the latest software version, I minimise vulnerabilities that could be exploited by attackers.

I consider a full factory reset when buying a second-hand phone a necessity to protect my privacy and security. Without taking this step, I leave open the possibility that hidden applications or residual data could compromise my personal information. Though the process may seem technical at first, I find that it is designed to be user-friendly and is supported by detailed guides from manufacturers and reputable sellers alike. The cost of a reset, in terms of time and effort, is minimal compared to the potential risk of identity theft, unauthorised tracking, or other invasive actions.

I remind myself that my personal data is precious, and taking the time to secure my device is an investment in my privacy.

8.5 Real Life Cases and Lessons Learnt

There was a case where a used phone was found to contain preinstalled software that could track its location, messages, and calls. Similar stories, shared on online security platforms and confirmed by mobile security experts, remind me that such invasive software is a real threat.[51]

There was also a case from overseas where someone bought a second-hand phone from an online marketplace, only to later discover that his personal data was being accessed remotely. The buyer noticed that his contacts and messages were inexplicably being transmitted to an unknown server. Even though the seller claimed that the phone had been "wiped," the reset had not been performed properly. This serves as a stark reminder to me that I should never rely solely on the seller's assurance; performing the reset myself is the only way to be sure.

Remember: *"Past owners' shadows linger; reset to extinguish danger."*

I've also participated in discussions on various forums where other users share their concerns about the risks associated with used devices. Many of us agree that a properly reset phone minimises the risks of inherited spyware or unwanted tracking. However, some of them caution that if any remnants of the previous owner's data remain, the risk can be significant. I'm also reminded that issues like activation locks can complicate matters; even a properly reset phone can be rendered useless if it remains linked to the previous owner's account[52].

---

51. Muncaster (2023), which outlines risks posed by unverified pre-owned devices and underscores the necessity of factory resets to erase residual data, including hidden tracking software.

52. In an Apple Community forum discussion, user *Kappy* (2020) emphasises that while factory-resetting a used iPhone mitigates spyware risks, activation lock tied to the previous owner's Apple ID can render the device unusable.

Reflecting on various real-life cases, the recurring theme is the necessity of ensuring that the device I purchase is as close to a "new" phone as possible. I always perform a full factory reset, followed by immediate software updates and security checks, because this is the only way to achieve a truly clean slate. Even if a seller claims that the phone has been cleaned, I don't take their word at face value. I always take the initiative to perform the reset myself.

The real-life examples I've come across, both from overseas and locally, underline for me that the potential dangers of preowned phones that are not properly reset are very real. These risks are not just theoretical but have led to serious financial and personal consequences. By learning from these cases, I adopt the necessary precautions and avoid falling victim to deceptive practices when buying a used phone.

8.6 Guidelines and Best Practices

Before I buy a used phone, I always research where I'm purchasing it from. I look for reputable retailers or certified refurbished programs, and I check customer reviews on trusted websites and local forums to gauge the experiences of others. A seller with a high rating is more likely to provide a device that has been properly reset and inspected. If I'm dealing with a private seller on an online marketplace, I exercise extra caution. I ask for detailed photos, proof of a recent reset, and even the original purchase receipt to verify the seller's legitimacy. I also prefer sellers who offer return policies[53] or warranties, which gives me peace of mind. For instance, many certified outlets now offer a minimum 12-month warranty and risk-free return periods.

Another non-negotiable step is performing the reset myself. The process is usually found in the settings menu under system options. I follow the instructions in the settings menu to restore the device to its original

53. Purchasing preowned devices from certified retailers or verified sellers with warranties and return policies significantly reduces risks (Quotient, n.d.).

state. This step eliminates any residual data or hidden software that might compromise my privacy. I immediately update the operating system after the reset. Installing the latest software to ensure that I have the latest security patches.

Once I have my phone, I do a thorough physical inspection, checking for any signs of tampering, such as unusual screws, scratches around the ports, or any modifications that don't look standard. If I see anything suspicious, I'm extra cautious. A reputable seller's device should appear as close to its original condition as possible.

After I perform a full factory reset and update the software, I set up the device entirely from scratch. I create my user account, set a strong and unique password, and enable biometric security features, such as fingerprint or facial recognition, if available. I also make sure to enable two-factor authentication wherever possible. This way, I can be sure that I have control over all the security settings.

To add another layer of protection, I install reputable security applications and run periodic antivirus and anti-malware scans. I rely on these programs to alert me if they detect any unusual activity or potential threats. While a properly reset device should be clean, I make it a point to run a security scan periodically, as a good habit.

I also monitor my phone's battery usage, data consumption, and overall performance, since any unexplained changes could indicate a hidden threat. I closely monitor the activity logs to make sure there are no unusual processes running in the background. If I notice that the battery suddenly drains much faster than expected or if there are unusual spikes in data usage, it might be time to run another security check. I appreciate that many devices now offer activity logs that help me monitor what is running in the background.

By following these guidelines, I create multiple layers of defence against the risks associated with buying a pre-owned phone. I remind myself that my personal data is highly valuable, and investing a little extra time to secure my device is well worth it.

8.7 Conclusion

Securing a second-hand phone requires diligence and a proactive approach. A full factory reset, though often overlooked, is the most effective step in ensuring that no traces of previous ownership or malicious software remain. While the appeal of a cost-effective, high-quality device is understandable, it is crucial to acknowledge the hidden risks that can come with purchasing preowned phones. Whether it's location tracking, unauthorised access to messages, or hidden spyware, taking the time to properly reset the device is an investment in both your security and peace of mind.

Takeaway: A Fresh Start for Ultimate Security

✓ Act Now:

- Always perform a full factory reset yourself on a used phone before use.
- Install the latest operating system and update security patches immediately after the reset.
- Physical inspection for any signs of tampering or unusual modifications.

✖ Stop This:

- Relying solely on a seller's statement that the phone is clean.
- Logging into sensitive accounts before you are sure the device is safe.

Core Defence:

- Every used phone must be considered a potential security risk until it has been restored to its original factory condition.
- Taking the simple steps above to ensure that hidden software or residual data does not compromise your privacy.

PART 09

DIGITAL HAZARDS OF GAMBLING AND ADULT CONTENT

Gambling and adult content scams thrive in the darker corners of Malaysia's digital ecosystem, preying on vulnerabilities and fostering societal harm. These deceptive practices erode financial stability and social responsibility, demanding proactive measures to shield communities from their corrosive influence.

9.1 Hidden Dangers in the Digital World

The internet is a wonderful tool that connects me to people all over the globe. It provides us with access to information, entertainment, and opportunities that were once unimaginable. However, along with these benefits come hidden dangers that are not always obvious at first glance. Many websites that offer adult content or gambling entertainment may seem harmless, but they can harbour malicious software that we never asked for. These sites often operate in a way that disguises their true intent. Pop-ups or warning messages may not appear immediately; instead, dangerous programs are often hidden deep within the website's code. These programs might be designed to monitor our online behaviour, capture personal data, or even take control of our devices[54].

To truly grasp how these hidden dangers manifest, let's imagine browsing on a website that appears to offer free entertainment. Unbeknownst to us, malware is installed on the device and quietly begins tracking our actions. It might not be immediately apparent that something is amiss until we start to notice unusual behaviour, such as sluggish performance or an unexpected battery drain. The risk increases if we use the same device to access sensitive information like our banking details. Cyber attackers can be highly creative in embedding their programs within a website's design, and it is not

---

[54]. A 2024 study by Chris Stokel-Walker found that visiting adult or gambling websites doubles the risk of malware infection, with such sites often distributing crypto miners, trojans, and hacking tools through hidden code, highlighting the hidden dangers of seemingly benign online activities (*Stokel-Walker*, 2024).

uncommon for users to be completely unaware that they have become a victim of such malware.

This hidden threat is a reminder that the digital world can sometimes be as dangerous as it is convenient. Similar to how a seemingly friendly stranger may have hidden motives, some websites hide their real intentions behind attractive interfaces. This deceptive approach has led many victims to suffer significant losses due to unauthorised access to personal information. Recognising these dangers is our first step in protecting ourselves against them.

9.2 Platform Operations to Deceive Users

Many gambling or adult content platforms operate by luring users in with promises of entertainment, free access, or quick rewards. These websites, often disguised as legitimate gaming hubs[55] or exclusive content portals, are designed to be visually appealing and to create a sense of urgency that compels us to click. Once we are on the site, the danger begins. Gambling platforms flash fake "jackpot" alerts, and adult content sites often auto-play videos to distract users. Meanwhile, hidden scripts run in the background, redirecting our browser or installing malicious programs that harvest our personal data and track our online behaviour.

These methods are often very subtle. The website may allow us to browse normally while silently installing programs on our device. For instance, if we use a device that also provides access to our bank accounts, the risk of such malware is magnified. These programs can monitor our keystrokes or take snapshots of the screen, making it easy for cyber criminals to steal sensitive information, such as our passwords and bank details.

Remember: *"Jackpot flashes blind eyes; silent scripts steal lives."*

---

55. *Sivesind* (2024) warns that compromised gambling apps, disguised as legitimate platforms, exploit enticing promises (e.g., high returns) to install malware and steal data. This mirroring the deceptive tactics of websites mimicking reputable hubs to lure unsuspecting users.

The deceptive techniques used by these websites may include pop-up prompts that ask us to click on various links. These prompts are often designed in a way that disguises their real purpose. They may appear as system warnings or notifications that require immediate action. If we click in haste, we may inadvertently confirm the installation of malware without realising it. In many cases, the website will simply continue to load even after we have attempted to close the page, and by that time, it is too late[56]. The malicious program is already in place and working quietly in the background, ready to collect our information and potentially compromise our privacy.

This modern form of deception exploits the trust that we sometimes place in seemingly reputable websites. Just because a website looks professional or familiar does not guarantee its safety. The methods used by these deceptive online schemes are constantly evolving, which makes it challenging for users to keep up with the latest threats. That is why we must always maintain a healthy dose of scepticism when browsing online, especially on websites that seem too good to be true.

9.3 The Motivation Behind Visiting Risky Websites

Even though we may be aware of the potential dangers, we sometimes visit gambling or adult content websites for various reasons. Often, it is a combination of curiosity and convenience that draws us in. The lure of free entertainment or the promise of exclusive content can be very strong, particularly when the website is marketed in a way that downplays the risks[57]. The idea of gaining access to content that

---

56. Scam pop-up ads often mimic legitimate tech companies, using urgent warnings (e.g., fake virus alerts, system crashes) to trick users into downloading malware, hijacking browsers, or divulging sensitive data, and risks are compounded by malicious sites that persist even after closing the page (*Trend Micro*, 2025).

57. *Clark* (2024) highlights that teens' easy access to online gambling platforms (often resembling games and marketed with enticing bonuses) exploits curiosity and underestimation of risks, compounded by parental unawareness and inadequate regulation, mirroring broader vulnerabilities in high-risk online behaviours.

is not readily available on more reputable sites can be very enticing. Sometimes, we become accustomed to a certain type of browsing behaviour and do not fully consider the consequences of visiting these sites.

Economic incentives can also drive this behaviour. The temptation to save money sometimes outweighs the abstract risks. Websites promising free access to premium content (e.g., pirated sports streams or adult platforms) exploit our financial constraints, offering short-term benefits that obscure long-term threats like malware infections. When we access free streaming sites, we may ignore hidden costs, such as compromised credit card details, until irreversible damage occurs.

Social factors also play a role in our decisions. We may feel the pull of online communities where friends or peers encourage us to explore these sites without fully discussing or disclosing the risks involved. Sometimes we give in to peer pressure or the urge to join a group that takes risks for fun. This herd mentality, which I have experienced in closed online groups sharing links to 'exclusive' gambling forums or adult content hubs, sometimes masks the collective vulnerability to malware. It is easy to assume that having technical knowledge offers sufficient protection, leading to an underestimation of the danger. There may be a belief that malicious websites can be easily identified or that a device is secure enough to withstand hidden threats.

The decision to visit these websites is often not made lightly. Deep down, I am aware of the potential consequences of exposing myself to malware and malicious software. However, the instant gratification and promise of excitement can sometimes override my caution. I have experienced instances where, in a hurry or while distracted, I click on links without fully understanding what I am doing. Once the process starts, it can be very difficult to stop the installation of malware or to undo the damage that has already been done.

I recall a situation where I was looking for a quick way to watch a popular movie online. I came across a website that offered the movie for free and decided to give it a try. Despite my awareness of the potential risks, I clicked on the link, and within moments, a series of redirects and pop-up messages began to appear. Before I knew it, malware had been installed on my device, and I was left wondering how a simple click led to a major compromise of my personal information[58].

Figure 9.1 Adult content and gambling ads pop up on online drama websites.

9.4 Case Studies of Deceptive Practices

The dangers of these deceptive practices are not just theoretical. There was an incident in another country where a user unintentionally installed a hidden monitoring program from a website that promised free streaming of a popular television show. This tactic was also used in a global malvertising campaign targeting illegal streaming platforms, where hackers embedded malicious ads within movie frames to redirect

[58] *Puig* (2019) warns that illegal streaming apps and add-ons, often marketed as gateways to free movies or TV shows, are frequently laced with malware capable of hijacking devices, stealing financial data, and compromising entire home networks, and these risks are exemplified by users unknowingly installing malicious programs through seemingly harmless clicks.

users to GitHub or Discord, triggering multi-stage malware downloads. These payloads, disguised as legitimate software via forged certificates, stole cryptocurrency wallets and passwords, and even enabled the remote control of devices[59]. In this case, the malicious program went undetected for weeks while it quietly collected sensitive data.

Similarly, a 2024 study by YouGov revealed that over one-third of Malaysian viewers, access pirated sports streams, which exposes them to risks, such as credential theft and botnet infections. Illegal streaming platforms in Malaysia often mimic legitimate services, embedding malicious ads that redirect users to malware-laden GitHub repositories or phishing sites. For example, Android TV boxes may come preloaded with unauthorised apps (similar to Singapore's banned SVI Cloud and EVPad models) that are sold online, with 44% of apps found to contain malware[60]. These devices, often marketed as "free access" solutions, enable cybercriminals to hijack home networks, steal financial data, and remotely control compromised devices.

In such cases, victims remain oblivious to the associated risks, allowing the damage to persist until the malware's eventual discovery. These incidents have reinforced the need for the safety measures I now follow.

9.5 Practical Maintenance Measures for Digital Safety

A key aspect of protecting ourselves is understanding how cyber criminals adapt to our online habits. They often study common browsing behaviours and target those habits specifically. For instance, if they are aware that I visit specific websites on devices that are also used

---

59. *Naprys* (2025) details a global malvertising campaign targeting illegal streaming platforms, where hackers embedded malicious ads in movie frames to redirect users to GitHub and Discord, deploying multi-stage malware disguised as legitimate software via forged certificates, for stealing cryptocurrency wallets and passwords, and enabling the remote control of devices.

60. Users of illegal streaming platforms and Android TV boxes in Southeast Asia face significantly higher risks of malware infections and financial scams, with 44% of apps on such devices containing malicious code (*Hamzah*, 2024).

for sensitive tasks, they tailor their programs to take advantage of this situation. This adaptability means that what worked as a deceptive tactic a few years ago might not be effective today, and new methods are continually being developed. As a result, I stay informed about the latest trends in cybersecurity because it is crucial for my safety online.

To counter this evolving threat, I have adopted proactive defences. If I access gambling or adult content platforms, I ensure that I use a dedicated device solely for these activities. Unregulated betting sites often host aggressive adware targeting payment details, so I make sure that this device is not linked to any of my sensitive accounts. I have learnt that by using a dedicated device solely for entertainment purposes, I minimise the chance that malware can access sensitive information stored on my primary devices.

I also make it a habit to regularly inspect the list of applications installed on my devices. Just as I would perform regular maintenance on my car to ensure its smooth operation, I treat my digital devices with the same care. I set aside time (perhaps once a month) to go through my phone or computer and check for any unfamiliar or unnecessary apps. If I notice an application that has access to features that are not necessary for its function, I immediately revoke those permissions or remove the app[61]. I am especially cautious with apps that request permissions like access to my camera when it isn't needed.

In addition, regular password changes are essential for protecting my personal information. I make sure to create strong and unique passwords for every account, avoiding easily guessed information, such as birthdays or common words. I opt for complex combinations of letters, numbers, and symbols, and I avoid reusing passwords across different sites. Even in the absence of any suspicious activity, I proactively change my

---

61. *Doffman* (2024) highlights widespread Android app permission abuse, with popular shopping platforms like Lazada requesting up to 17 dangerous permissions (e.g., camera/microphone access, location tracking).

passwords every few months to deter cyber attackers. If I ever suspect that my device may have been compromised, I promptly change my passwords for all sensitive accounts.

Along with this, I clear my device's cache files and browsing history regularly to maintain my digital safety. Over time, remnants of data can accumulate and may be exploited by malicious programs to extract information about my online habits. I make it a habit to clear this data periodically through my browser's settings, thus removing any traces that could be used to piece together a profile of my activities.

Ultimately, creating multiple layers of protection is key to keeping my digital life secure. Even if I accidentally visit a gambling or adult content website, these additional steps help mitigate the damage. It's not about living in fear of every click but about being prepared and taking sensible precautions. A little extra effort in maintaining my device and monitoring my online activity goes a long way in ensuring that my personal information remains safe.

9.6 Conclusion

As we move forward, it is essential that we, as a nation, continue to raise awareness about the dangers of gambling and adult content scams. By sharing knowledge and taking collective action, we can protect the well-being of our society and foster a safer, more responsible digital environment. It is our shared responsibility to safeguard the future of our nation by ensuring that these harmful practices do not take root in our communities. Let us stand together to make Malaysia a safer place for everyone online.

Takeaway: Isolate Risks for Safe Browsing

✓ Act Now:

- Use separate dedicated devices to browse gambling or adult content.
- Update antivirus software regularly, clear cache and history, and review app permissions.
- Create and frequently update unique passwords for accounts linked to high-risk platforms.

✖ Stop This:

- Browsing risky websites, such as gambling or adult content on your primary device where you store personal or financial data.
- Clicking on suspicious links, pop-ups, or any prompts that look inappropriate.

🛡 Core Defence:

- Isolate high-risk browsing activities from your everyday devices.

PART 10

NAVIGATING THE MAZE OF AI SCAMS

Artificial intelligence (AI) reshapes industries and daily life, yet its rapid adoption introduces unprecedented risks. AI-driven scams now target unsuspecting Malaysians, exploiting technological trust to commit scams and identity theft. Understanding these threats is essential to harnessing AI's benefits while safeguarding our nation's digital future.

10.1 Technology's Double-Edged Sword

I remember the first time I truly grasped the power of AI; it was both exhilarating and intimidating. This transformative tool had the potential to change lives for the better, yet I soon discovered that it also held the potential to wreak havoc in unscrupulous hands. I have always been fascinated by technology, watching it slowly permeate every aspect of life, from education and business to the way we connect with one another. When AI began emerging as a transformative force, it felt like stepping into a new dimension of possibilities.

I vividly recall my first encounter with an AI-powered virtual assistant. I was amazed at how it could understand my spoken language and provide meaningful responses almost instantly. That moment ignited a burning curiosity within me, not just to understand how AI works but also to explore how it was reshaping our lives. Over time, as I witnessed AI's rapid advancement, I realised that alongside its many benefits, there was a darker, less-discussed side, which is the rise of AI-driven scams.

Every technological breakthrough carries inherent risks. Similar to how the invention of the telephone revolutionised communication and simultaneously gave rise to phone scams, AI presents both advantages and disadvantages. On one hand, AI offers tremendous promise in fields like healthcare, education, and business, transforming lives with innovative solutions. On the other hand, its powerful qualities, such as adaptability and the ability to mimic human behaviour, make it an ideal instrument for scammers to manipulate and exploit individuals and organisations[62].

Gone are the days when a simple phone call or email would be enough to dupe someone. I have read about scams where AI was used to create counterfeit documents like fake passports, driver's licences, and academic certificates. Such deceptions can have serious implications for national security and public safety, as the sophistication of these forgeries (enabled by AI's advanced image processing) makes them increasingly difficult to detect.

Yet the danger is not solely technological. One of the most disconcerting aspects of AI scams is how they exploit human psychology. As I pieced together various scam tactics, I realised that their success isn't only due to technological prowess; it is also intricately linked to the quirks and vulnerabilities of human nature. Our innate desire to trust, be connected, and dream of easy solutions are all factors that scammers manipulate to their advantage. They even fabricate social proof, creating illusions that "everyone else is doing it" to pressure victims into compliance[63]. Our tendency to respond to authority, seek quick gains, follow the crowd, and overly trust familiar sources makes us particularly susceptible to these scams.

These lessons have shaped my approach to digital interactions. I now make it a point to verify every communication, to educate those around me, and to remain ever cautious in the face of technology's alluring promises. Understanding these scams is vital to safeguarding our digital lives, and the wake-up call they provide has inspired me to delve deeper, not only to protect myself but also to help others recognise the hidden dangers behind seemingly legitimate digital interactions. To fully grasp

---

62. The revolutionary qualities of AI, including adaptability and sophistication, are exploited by criminal networks to execute scams (Reuters, 2025).

63. Scammers exploit social proof by fabricating scenarios where victims believe others have already complied, leveraging our instinct to conform to perceived group behaviour (Bisht, 2024).

how these threats manifest, we must examine the specific tactics scammers employ in the AI era.

10.2 AI-Powered Phishing Scams

In my deeper exploration of AI, I encountered numerous cases of elaborate phishing scams that combine modern techniques with emotional manipulation. In the past, phishing relied on generic emails to trick recipients into clicking on malicious links. Today, scammers use AI to craft highly personalised messages by scraping social media profiles for details, such as names, interests, and recent activities. With this information, they create emails that appear to come from trusted sources like banks or friends.

There was a case where a person nearly fell for an AI-generated phishing email mimicking our local bank. The email was so convincing. It mentioned the victim's recent transaction and even included his name in the greeting until a small inconsistency in the bank's name raised suspicions. This incident underscored how AI can lower our defences by exploiting our trust in familiar institutions.

Moreover, AI now enables scammers to automate and scale their operations dramatically. A scammer, who once manually sent deceptive emails to a few dozen victims a day, can now send personalised messages to millions in a matter of minutes. Algorithms analyse public data to tailor messages to each recipient's interests and vulnerabilities[64], making it incredibly difficult for even the most cautious individuals to detect a scam. I have followed cases where machine learning was used to send thousands of scam messages in a short time; these messages are often timed to coincide with events, such as tax deadlines or major public announcements.

---

64. AI-driven automation allows scammers to generate thousands of personalised phishing emails within minutes, exploiting both technological and psychological vulnerabilities (New York University, n. d.).

In addition to personalisation, scammers often create a false sense of urgency in order to bypass rational thought. There was a case involving a text message warning of a security breach in a victim's bank account, complete with AI-generated images of red alert symbols, urging immediate action. Despite the initial panic, the victim took a moment to verify the information and realised it was a scam. This tactic exploits our natural tendency to react quickly in moments of panic or anxiety.

Together, these examples illustrate how AI has transformed phishing scams into sophisticated operations that combine targeted personalisation with emotional manipulation, leaving even the most vigilant individuals vulnerable.

10.3 Deepfake Scams

Deepfake technology is one of the most unnerving applications of AI in scams. Using advanced machine learning algorithms, deepfakes create hyper-realistic videos of people saying or doing things they never actually did. I first encountered deepfakes during a cybersecurity seminar, where the presenter showed videos of political figures and celebrities uttering outrageous statements fabricated entirely by AI. These videos are nearly indistinguishable from real footage, immediately raising concerns about their potential misuse.

I began to worry that if deepfakes can manipulate public opinion or tarnish reputations, scammers could easily use them for financial scams. In 2024, Steve Harvey's voice was cloned by AI to promote a deceptive scheme promising government funds. Harvey, whose likeness has been exploited in scams at an all-time high, now advocates for legislation such as the No Fakes Act to penalise AI-driven scams[65]. This

---

[65]. AI-generated voice clones of Steve Harvey promoted deceptive government fund schemes, exploiting trust in public figures to deceive victims at scale, as Harvey, whose likeness was abused in scams reaching 'an all-time high,' advocates for the No Fakes Act to penalise AI-driven scams (Gold, 2025).

incident exemplifies how even trusted public figures can be weaponised by scammers to deceive victims on a massive scale.

Figure 10.1 Deepfake videos featuring Tom Cruise's likeness went viral on social media.

I was both impressed and disturbed by how convincingly deepfake technology can create illusions. This experience underscores the need for robust verification processes and the importance of questioning even the most seemingly authentic communications.

10.4 Vishing Exploits in the Digital Age

In today's digital age, voice remains a highly trusted communication channel. The popularity of vishing, or voice-based phishing, has allowed scammers to take advantage of our inherent trust in voices. They often impersonate loved ones, such as children or family members, using phone calls to convince victims that the caller is genuine. By carefully mimicking familiar tones and speech patterns, these scammers dramatically increase their chances of deceiving unsuspecting individuals.

There was a case where an AI-generated voice impersonated a senior citizen's son, calling a parent and claiming to be in jail after a car accident. The voice was so realistic that the father believed his son was in danger, even handing over $25,000 to scammers posing as lawyers and Uber drivers[66]. The voice clone, coupled with urgent threats of legal consequences, left no time for scepticism. This incident demonstrated how vishing manipulates familial trust, exploiting fear and urgency to bypass rational judgement. It also highlighted how even a momentary lapse in verifying identities can lead to devastating financial losses.

This incident serves as a stark reminder that, as we increasingly rely on voice communications, our natural trust in loved ones' voices can be weaponised, leading to severe consequences. It also made me question how urgency and emotional manipulation override caution and scepticism, even in the most cautious individuals.

10.5 Fake Crypto Investment Scams

One area that has seen explosive growth is the use of AI in promoting fake investment schemes, particularly in the crypto space. Scammers exploit public fascination with AI to tout automated trading algorithms and crypto-asset strategies promising "guaranteed returns" or "huge profits" through bots and trade signals. I have seen numerous online advertisements and social media posts mimicking these claims, often amplified by influencers to target vulnerable investors during economic uncertainty. These scams prey on the allure of rapid wealth

---

66. Scammers used AI-generated voice cloning to impersonate a senior citizen's son, fabricating a car accident and urgent legal threats to manipulate the father into wiring $25,000 to fake lawyers and Uber drivers, exploiting familial trust and urgency to bypass verification (Pollina, 2024).

accumulation with minimal risk—a narrative that regulators warn is a hallmark of scams[67].

I once attended a webinar that claimed to reveal the secret behind an "AI-powered crypto bot" capable of doubling investments overnight. The presentation was slick and filled with impressive charts and graphs generated by AI tools. However, I soon learnt that behind the glittering facade was nothing more than a carefully orchestrated pyramid scheme. Many investors lost significant sums of money, and the scam eventually collapsed, leaving behind a trail of disillusioned victims. This experience reinforced the critical need for scepticism and thorough research before trusting any investment opportunities that seem too good to be true.

10.6 The Allure of Fake Opportunities

In today's interconnected world, scammers exploit AI to flood online marketplaces with fake reviews and ratings, creating a false sense of trust through meticulously crafted, overly positive feedback. These AI-generated reviews often mimic authentic user testimonials, complete with fabricated purchase histories and counterfeit product images, making it nearly impossible for unsuspecting buyers to distinguish real from deceptive.

I have encountered cases where individuals fall prey to scams from a seller with a flawless profile on online marketplaces. In one instance, scammers used AI-generated profiles to sell counterfeit goods at attractive prices. The deals appeared to be too good to be true. The seller's profile was impeccably designed with AI-enhanced detailed product images and positive reviews praising the "fast shipping" and "authentic quality." However, despite the payment, the goods never arrived. This incident underscores how AI not only amplifies deception but also erodes the very mechanisms we rely on to verify legitimacy online.

---

67. Scammers leverage AI-driven algorithms and social media to promote deceptive crypto schemes promising unrealistic returns (Commodity Futures Trading Commission (CFTC), 2024).

The danger lies in the scalability of these scams. A single scammer can deploy AI tools to generate thousands of fake profiles and reviews within minutes, targeting platforms from e-commerce sites to social media marketplaces. What makes these schemes particularly insidious is their ability to exploit human psychology because we are wired to trust consensus, and a wall of positive reviews (even if fabricated) can override rational scepticism.[68]

This serves as a stark reminder that, in the age of AI, even everyday online interactions can harbour the threat of AI-powered scams. The line between authentic opportunity and sophisticated scam has never been thinner.

10.7 The Malaysian Digital Landscape

Understanding these new scam techniques has been both enlightening and alarming. As I explored further, I began to see clear patterns that reveal how AI scams exploit our inherent cognitive biases. Many scammers take advantage of our natural tendency to trust technology, assuming that if something is powered by advanced technology, it must be trustworthy. They craft high-tech, polished schemes that mimic reputable institutions, making it incredibly challenging to distinguish genuine communications from deceptive ones. Cognitive biases, such as authority bias and confirmation bias, leave us particularly vulnerable; we often ignore red flags if a scam aligns with our pre-existing beliefs[69], which dulls our awareness of warning signs, especially when scammers are armed with cutting-edge AI tools.

In Malaysia, these vulnerabilities are amplified by a unique blend of rapid digital adoption and varied levels of digital literacy. Many

---

68. Scammers leverage AI to flood platforms with fake reviews and profiles, exploiting human trust in consensus to manipulate purchasing decisions (Federal Trade Commission, 2024).

69. Authority bias drives compliance with perceived authorities like banks, while confirmation bias leads victims to selectively accept deceptive information (Bal, 2024).

Malaysians eagerly embrace new technologies, yet this enthusiasm often comes without full awareness of the associated security risks. In my interactions with local business owners and community leaders, I frequently hear, "How can we enjoy the benefits of AI without falling victim to these scams?" This pressing question underscores the urgent need for awareness and education.

Remember: *"Digital leaps need rooted feet; educate to defeat."*

While digital advancements bring numerous opportunities, they also render our community more susceptible to cyber threats, particularly AI-powered scams. Scammers can harness the very tools designed to enhance our lives, exploiting both our technological trust and cultural factors. In communities where digital literacy is still evolving, the sophistication of AI scams can be especially intimidating, as unbridled trust in modern systems may lead to dangerous complacency.

Moreover, the consequences of these scams extend beyond individual losses. Economically, large-scale scams can destabilise markets, affect investor confidence, and impact national economies. Socially, victims often suffer embarrassment, anxiety, and isolation, with some withdrawing from online activities altogether for fear of being targeted again. This self-imposed digital isolation not only limits personal growth but also hinders the overall progress of our increasingly digital society.

Together, these insights emphasise the importance of a balanced approach to digital engagement—one that embraces innovation while fostering a culture of scepticism, vigilance, and mutual support. Recognising both the benefits and inherent risks of AI has become a personal mission, driving me to learn everything I can about these scams and share that knowledge to help safeguard our digital future.

10.8 Uniting Against AI-Driven Threats

The first and most important step in preventing AI scams is education. Building a culture of awareness within our personal circles and at the community level is essential. I make it a point to share what I learn with my family, friends, and colleagues, because when people understand how these scams operate, they are less likely to fall prey to them. In Malaysia, where digital transformation is rapid and a young, tech-savvy population is emerging, there is an urgent need for widespread public education. By integrating digital literacy into the education system, we can empower the next generation to critically assess information, question what they see, and verify before they trust. Following Malaysia's National Anti-Scam Education Programme, which integrates scam awareness into school curriculum, a similar approach should be adopted for AI-specific risks[70]. Educating both the public and the next generation about the benefits and dangers of AI will help build a society that is innovative, resilient, and better equipped to resist the manipulative tactics of AI scammers. The fight against AI scams does not require sacrificing innovation for security, or vice versa. It requires a dual commitment, which includes advancing ethical AI development while building proactive defences, akin to how medical science continuously adapts vaccines to counter viral evolution.

Beyond personal education, I believe that government agencies, financial institutions, and tech companies must collaborate to create a multilayered defence system. This system should align with frameworks like the expanded NIST AI Risk Management Framework, incorporating standardised data "nutrition labels" to track AI model inputs and outputs and robust digital identity solutions to combat scams. Early warning mechanisms, real-time monitoring, and rapid response frameworks are critical to address emerging threats. No single entity

---

[70]. Malaysia's National Anti-Scam Education Programme, developed by the Ministry of Education with cybersecurity experts, advocates integrating scam awareness into school curricula to empower youth against scams (Beh, 2025).

can combat these challenges alone; it requires a concerted effort that combines technological innovation with proactive regulation. Regulatory coordination across federal and state levels, alongside international partnerships, is essential to avoid fragmentation and ensure cohesive oversight[71]. The fight against AI scams is not an individual battle but a collective endeavour that demands a shared commitment to vigilance, education, and mutual support.

By learning from each other's experiences and pooling our resources, we can develop localised guidelines, more effective security tools, and policies to safeguard our digital lives, ultimately reducing the prevalence of AI scams. Fostering such networks, particularly in Malaysia, is crucial. Initiatives like the Youths IRL Fellowship, which empowers diverse communities to share insights with policymakers, demonstrate how knowledge-sharing can create a formidable barrier against scammers[72]. Together, we can advocate for stronger regulations, build a digital environment that is both innovative and secure, and create a culture where knowledge is freely shared. Collaborative efforts will diminish the threat of AI scams and ensure that the benefits of AI are realised without sacrificing our security and trust. I remain committed to supporting initiatives aimed at enhancing digital security at a national level and encourage everyone to play their part in this collective effort.

10.9 Conclusion

As Malaysians, we must stay vigilant against AI-driven scams that pose a serious risk to our personal security and the integrity of our digital economy. By fostering awareness and encouraging responsible use of AI, we contribute to building a safer and more resilient society. It is

---

71. The U.S. Treasury advocates for regulatory coordination, AI risk management frameworks, and digital identity standards to address AI-driven scams and cybersecurity gaps in the financial sector (U.S. Department of the Treasury, 2024).

72. Initiatives like Malaysia's Youths IRL Fellowship, part of the Online Safety Campaign by Ratio: Cause and partners, exemplify collaborative efforts to bridge grassroots insights with policy development in combating AI scams (Tan, 2025).

our collective responsibility to not only understand these threats but also to support the efforts of governments, businesses, and educators in combating this growing issue. Together, we can safeguard the digital space for future generations, ensuring that technological advancements remain a force for good in our society.

Takeaway: Outsmart AI Deception

✓ Act Now:

- Verify every AI-driven message using independent channels.
- Use secondary confirmation for urgent requests.
- Stay updated on emerging AI scam tactics.

✖ Stop This:

- Trusting hyper-personalised or deepfake content without cross-checking it first.
- Reacting immediately to pressure or “guaranteed” opportunities.

🛡 Core Defence:

- Always verify AI-generated communications with a sceptical eye before taking action.

SUMMARY

All scams in Malaysia operate in the same way, with constant variations. The most common tools used by scammers are fake phone calls, text messages, and even the most popular AI tools that impersonate the voices of family members. Scams are perpetrated when we panic or believe false information too quickly, leading to irrational thinking and judgment. Although Malaysian law has clearly stipulated that scammers are criminals, we must always remain vigilant to avoid becoming victims of scams.

Scams can hide in apps like wedding invitations or cleaning services. Once people click the install button without thinking, these apps reveal their true intent to steal our banking information in the blink of an eye. In 2023 alone, such scams have caused serious losses of more than RM18 million in Malaysia. Seeing how easily fake apps can drain savings, I now download apps only from the official app store that comes with my phone and carefully check what permissions they request.

We often choose to use online banking after connecting to public Wi-Fi for the sake of convenience and saving time, but we subconsciously ignore the huge risks that this simple behaviour exposes us to. After reading some news reports about public Wi-Fi scams, I now habitually turn on the mobile data purchased from the telecommunications provider when I go out. I also use separate browsers for daily browsing and banking. After completing financial transactions, I always log out manually and never leave the session open.

Data breaches in Malaysia have become increasingly severe, with hackers targeting outdated routers and corporate servers to steal sensitive information, then extorting high ransoms by threatening to expose the data. Therefore, to mitigate these risks, enterprises should prioritise regular system updates on aging network infrastructures, and implement encrypted offsite backups on critical data to reduce the hackers' chances of attack.

Although the popularity of cashless payments has brought many conveniences to our daily lives, it also hides many risks. Scammers will quietly replace the store's QR code when we are not paying attention or show the merchant a fake payment interface on the mobile phone screen when paying. Therefore, I suggest that store owners use soundboxes that can loudly announce the amount of payment to prevent such scam cases from happening.

For fake websites that imitate real bank addresses to deceive victims' trust and money, I would first carefully check the domain and subdomain of the link, and then use MYNIC | WHOIS to determine whether the website is suspicious.

In our daily work, scammers use fake emails to trick company employees into sending them money. In 2024, a logistics company in Johor lost RM320,000 because it failed to double-check the authenticity of the email with its overseas business partners. After this incident was reported, my employees now call to confirm the payment request before making the transaction.

The chances of spyware being hidden inside a second-hand phone offered by random sellers online are very high, so I always choose to buy second-hand phones from trustworthy stores and reset them to factory settings myself.

Gambling or adult website pages often have ads that induce users to download illegal applications, which is one of the channels used by scammers to spread viruses. Therefore, I recommend that those who still insist on visiting such high-risk websites use a separate mobile phone to protect their main device.

Nowadays, the number of scams using AI videos or the voices of family members or bosses is increasing. If I feel something is not right, I will call the other party to confirm the authenticity. At the same time, I think stricter laws should be implemented to punish these crimes so that everyone can learn from them.

Combating scams in Malaysia requires a collective effort. Personal protection can start with simple, practical steps, such as using strong, unique passwords and avoiding suspicious links.

For companies, regular mandatory training for employees and prompt updates or repairs to outdated systems are essential safeguards.

At the national level, the government is strengthening anti-scam laws and working proactively with international counterparts to track down and prosecute scammers.

Educating children about online safety in schools and sharing scam alerts within community chat groups can all help towards making Malaysia a safer place.

REFERENCES

Foreword: A CEO's Scam Prevention Journey

1. Department of Statistics Malaysia. (2024, October 16). *Statistik Jenayah Malaysia 2024* [Crime Statistics Malaysia 2024]. pp. 166-167. https://storage.dosm.gov.my/crime/crime_2023.pdf.

Part 1: From Deceptive Roots to Collective Defences

1. Attorney General's Chambers of Malaysia. (2015). *Penal Code (Act 574)* (As at 1 January 2015), pp. 222-224. https://www.rcrc-resilience-southeastasia.org/wp-content/uploads/2017/12/Penal-Code-Act-574.pdf.
2. Paulas, R. (2015, March 4). The weird and fraudulent world of Catholic relics. *VICE.* https://www.vice.com/en/article/the-weird-and-fraudulent-world-of-catholic-relics-456/.
3. *Guangming Daily.* (2009, January 29). 金河广场找猎物 假和尚尼姑专诈游客 [Fake monks and nuns scam tourists at Sungei Wang Plaza]. https://guangming.com.my/%E9%87%91%E6%B2%B3%E5%BB%A3%E5%A0%B4%E6%89%BE%E7%8D%B5%E7%89%A9%E2%80%A7%E5%81%87%E5%92%8C%E5%B0%9A%E5%B0%BC%E5%A7%91%E5%B0%88%E8%A9%90%E9%81%8A%E5%AE%A2.
4. *Oriental Daily.* (2025, January 27). 误信最高19%回酬虚假投资 年轻商人损失逾16万令吉积蓄 [Misled by fake investment with 19% returns: Young businessman loses RM160,000 savings]. https://www.orientaldaily.com.my/news/society/2025/01/27/708720.

Part 2: Unmasking APK Scams

1. Kulkarni, S. (2024, November 4). SBI warns customers about this latest money fraud: What is APK fraud, tips to protect yourself. *The Economic Times.* https://economictimes.indiatimes.com/wealth/save/sbi-warns-customers-about-this-latest-money-fraud-what-is-apk-fraud-tips-to-protect-yourself/sbi-rewards-fraud/slideshow/114939622.cms.
2. *HDFC Bank.* (2025, January 6). Beware of the wedding invitation scam targeting WhatsApp users. https://www.hdfcbank.com/personal/resources/learning-centre/vigil-aunty/whatsapp-wedding-scam.

3. Roviello, M., & Strino, A. (2024, September 10). A new TrickMo saga: From banking trojan to victim's data leak. *Cleafy.* https://www.cleafy.com/cleafy-labs/a-new-trickmo-saga-from-banking-trojan-to-victims-data-leak.
4. *Secure Blink.* (2024, September 26). Necro Trojan's return: Infiltrating Google Play to target Android users. https://www.secureblink.com/threat-research/necro-trojan-s-return-infiltrating-google-play-to-target-android-users.
5. Ahmed, D. (2025, February 5). Banking malware uses live numbers to hijack OTPs, targeting 50,000 victims. *Hackread.* https://hackread.com/banking-malware-live-numbers-hijack-otp-50000-victims/.
6. Raja Rahim, R. N. (2024, June 6). Police records 67 cases of smartphone hacking through APK files with losses over RM1.1mil. *New Straits Times.* https://www.nst.com.my/news/nation/2024/06/1060175/police-records-67-cases-smartphone-hacking-through-apk-files-losses-over.
7. Lakshmanan, R. (2024, June 18). Singapore police extradites Malaysians linked to Android malware fraud. *The Hacker News.* https://thehackernews.com/2024/06/singapore-police-extradites-malaysians.html.
8. *The Economic Times.* (2024, November 13). WhatsApp fake wedding scam can steal all your money with one message — How it works and how to stay safe. https://economictimes.indiatimes.com/magazines/panache/whatsapp-fake-wedding-scam-can-steal-all-your-money-with-one-message-how-it-works-and-how-to-stay-safe/articleshow/115266324.cms?from=mdr.

Part 3: The Silent Takeover in a Digital World

1. Hassan, M. S., & Haque, E. H. F. (2020, February 23). 'Bencana' Wi-Fi awam. *Harian Metro.* Retrieved from https://www.hmetro.com.my/utama/2020/02/547446/bencana-Wi-Fi-awam-metrotv.
2. Hui, X. (2023, April 26). Fortress of security: Creating a strong password to safeguard your account. *Exabytes.* Retrieved from https://www.exabytes.my/blog/create-strong-password-to-secure-account/.

Part 4: Battle Against Invisible Data Thieves

1. Tiong, J. (2018, January 29). 马来西亚再曝个人信息泄露案 [Malaysia faces second major personal data leak]. *Asia Times.* https://www.asiatimes.com.

my/2018/01/29/%E9%A9%AC%E6%9D%A5%E8%A5%BF%E4%BA%9A%E5%86%8D%E6%9B%9D%E4%B8%AA%E4%BA%BA%E4%BF%A1%E6%81%AF%E6%B3%84%E9%9C%B2%E6%A1%88/.

2. *Telekom Malaysia.* (2022, December 30). TM's addresses data breach of Unifi mobile customers contact information. https://tm.com.my/news/tm-addresses-data-breach-unifi-mobile-customers-contact-info.
3. *MyCERT.* (2024, December 26). Cyber incident quarterly summary report - Q3 2024. https://www.mycert.org.my/portal/advisory?id=SR-028.122024.
4. 曾丽全. (2024, December 4). 促通讯部查大马卡资料外泄 刘华才：需加强网络安全 [Urge Communications Ministry to investigate MyKad data leak: Need to strengthen cybersecurity]. *Oriental Daily.* https://www.orientaldaily.com.my/news/nation/2024/12/04/697428.
5. *Bernama.* (2024, December 5). JPN confirms no MyKad data breach detected. https://www.bernama.com/en/news.php?id=2371402.
6. AnuPriya. (2025, January 28). Massive data breach hits Asia Recruit Malaysia. *Cyber Press.* https://cyberpress.org/asia-recruit-malaysia-breach/.
7. *MyCERT.* (2025, February 27). Cyber Incident Quarterly Summary Report - Q4 2024. https://www.mycert.org.my/portal/advisory?id=SR-029.022025.

Part 5: Wallets in the Wild

1. Philips, A. (2019, October 30). Coca Cola launched the first digital wallet in 1997. *Twin Rock Partners.* https://www.twinrockpartners.com/coca-cola-launched-the-first-digital-wallet-in-1997/#:~:text=Coca%20Cola%20is%20credited%20with,text%20message%20on%20their%20cellphone.
2. *Visa Inc.* (2008, September 25). Visa and Nokia working together to deliver payment applications for next generation mobile devices. https://investor.visa.com/news/news-details/2008/Visa-and-Nokia-Working-Together-to-Deliver-Payment-Applications-for-Next-Generation-Mobile-Devices/default.aspx.
3. Gomes, V. (2022, February 28). E-wallet: Digital payments pivotal to Malaysia's financial services industry. *The Edge Malaysia.* https://theedgemalaysia.com/article/ewallet-digital-payments-pivotal-malaysias-financial-services-industry.

4. *Bank Negara Malaysia.* (2022). Jom berdigital dengan yakin. In Laporan Tahunan 2022 (Box Artikel 6). https://www.bnm.gov.my/documents/20124/10150308/ar2022_bm_box6.pdf.
5. *Oppotus.* (2025, February 13). Malaysia's e-wallet and digital banking usage in 2024: Going cashless reigning supreme. https://www.oppotus.com/malaysias-e-wallet-and-digital-banking-usage-in-2024/.
6. Tan, Z. Y. (2022, January 24). E-wallet: Cybersecurity: How much cash would you keep in your e-wallet? *The Edge Malaysia.* https://theedgemalaysia.com/article/ewallet-cybersecurity-how-much-cash-would-you-keep-your-ewallet.
7. Oh, E. (2023, December 6). Scammer replaces M'sia restaurant's payment QR code with his own, allegedly tricks several customers. *MS News.* https://mustsharenews.com/scammer-qr-code/.
8. *Harapan Madani.* (2023, November). 新型骗局！骗子随身带电子支付二维码 芙蓉咖啡厅被替换 [New scam alert! Scammers replace café QR codes in Seremban]. https://harapanmadani.com/%E6%96%B0%E5%9E%8B%E9%AA%97%E5%B1%80%EF%BC%81%E9%AA%97%E5%AD%90%E9%9A%8F%E8%BA%AB%E5%B8%A6%E7%94%B5%E5%AD%90%E6%94%AF%E4%BB%98%E4%BA%8C%E7%BB%B4%E7%A0%81-%E8%8A%99%E8%93%89%E5%92%96%E5%95%A1%E5%8E%85/.
9. 郭贞黎. (2024, July 13). 趁你忙 使诈术 防电子付款 骗吃喝 [Scammers exploit busy hours to deceive e-payment users]. *China Press.* https://kl.chinapress.com.my/20240713/%E8%B6%81%E4%BD%A0%E5%BF%99-%E4%BD%BF%E8%AF%88%E6%9C%AF-%E9%98%B2%E7%94%B5%E5%AD%90%E4%BB%98%E6%AC%BE-%E9%AA%97%E5%90%83%E5%96%9D/.
10. 温丽媚. (2021, June 24). 利用电子钱包假过账骗货　商家识破骗财伎俩 [Scammers use fake e-wallet receipts to cheat merchants]. *Oriental Daily.* https://www.orientaldaily.com.my/news/society/2021/06/24/420075.
11. Toyos, L. (2025, February 22). Chamber: Many cheated in e-wallet transactions. *Daily Express.* https://www.dailyexpress.com.my/news/252707/chamber-many-cheated-in-e-wallet-transactions/.

Part 6: Digital Impersonation and Its Victims

1. *Phishing.org.* (n.d.). History of phishing. https://www.phishing.org/history-of-phishing.

2. *MyCERT.* (2004, February 16). RHB Bank new phishing scam. https://mycert.org.my/portal/advisory?id=MA-068.022004#:~:text=http://www.rhbbank.com,antiphishing.org/phishing_archive.htm.
3. *MyCERT.* (2004, September 9). Latest CITIBANK phishing scam. https://www.mycert.org.my/portal/advisory?id=MA-082.092004.
4. Wahab, S., & Hisham, H. (2025, January 23). The mounting landscape of phishing scams in Malaysia. *The Malaysian Reserve.* https://themalaysianreserve.com/2025/01/23/the-mounting-landscape-of-phishing-scams-in-malaysia/.
5. Mamat, N. (2025, February 19). Malaysian police and local bank warn public about 'lottery scam'. *AFP Fact Check.* https://factcheck.afp.com/doc.afp.com.36XK88W.

Part 7: Email Threats in Corporate Environments

1. *Guinness World Records.* (n.d.). First email. https://www.guinnessworldrecords.com/world-records/first-email
2. Smith, G. (2024, December 10). Top phishing statistics for 2025: Latest figures and trends. *StationX.* https://www.stationx.net/phishing-statistics/.
3. Winder, D. (2020, May 4). This 20-year-old virus infected 50 million Windows computers in 10 days: Why the ILOVEYOU pandemic matters in 2020. *Forbes.* https://www.forbes.com/sites/daveywinder/2020/05/04/this-20-year-old-virus-infected-50-million-windows-computers-in-10-days-why-the-iloveyou-pandemic-matters-in-2020/.
4. *IBM.* (2023, April 4). What is business email compromise (BEC)? https://www.ibm.com/think/topics/business-email-compromise#:~:text=Business%20email%20compromise%2C%20or%20BEC,some%20of%20the%20costliest%20cyberattacks.
5. Shadiqe, J. (2024, June 26). Logistics company loses RM321,698.74 in 'business email compromise' scam. *New Straits Times.* https://www.nst.com.my/news/nation/2024/06/1068507/logistics-company-loses-rm32169874-business-email-compromise-scam.
6. People's Daily. (2016, November 28). 上海反电信诈骗中心半年成功劝阻4.9万人次上当 [Shanghai Anti-Telecom Fraud Center successfully dissuaded 49,000 people from being deceived in half a year]. *Ministry of Public Security of the People's Republic of China.* https://www.mps.gov.cn/n2255079/n4876594/n5104076/n5104080/c5556249/content.html.

Part 8: Securing Second-hand Phones

1. *Verizon.* (2023, February 14). How to choose a phone: Certified Pre-Owned vs. refurbished vs. pre-owned. https://www.verizon.com/articles/prepaid-and-cpo/certified-pre-owned-refurbished-and-used-phones-guide/.
2. Banerjee, G. (2022, December). Malaysia Used Smartphone Market Outlook to 2026F. *Ken Research.* https://www.kenresearch.com/industry-reports/malaysia-used-smartphone-market.
3. Bhutani, D. (2023, November 18). It's not enough to just factory reset an Android phone before selling it. *Android Authority.* https://www.androidauthority.com/data-recovery-after-android-factory-reset-3384980/.
4. Chmura, C., Hansen, B., Hargrove, D., & Jackson, J. (2019, September 4). Buying used smartphones: Save money, but be careful. *NBC Bay Area.* https://www.nbcbayarea.com/news/local/used-phone-shopping-do-this-first/1959598/.
5. Culbert, D. (2021, June 7). How secure is your refurbished phone? *Brilliance Security Magazine.* https://brilliancesecuritymagazine.com/cybersecurity/how-secure-is-your-refurbished-phone/.
6. Hill, S. (2024, September 19). How to Factory-Reset Your Phone Before You Sell It. *Wired.* https://www.wired.com/story/how-to-reset-your-phone-before-you-sell-it/.
7. Muncaster, P. (2023, December 9). Are pre-owned smartphones safe? How to choose a second-hand phone and avoid security risks. *We Live Security.* https://www.welivesecurity.com/en/mobile-security/are-preowned-smartphones-safe-how-choose-second-hand-phone-avoid-security-risks/.
8. Kappy. (2020, March 8). Re: Used iPhone security risk? [Online forum comment]. *Apple Support Community.* https://discussions.apple.com/thread/251173834?sortBy=rank.
9. Quotient. (n.d.). Why its worth buying second hand phones. *IQ Repairs.* https://iqrepairs.com/2572-2.

Part 9: Digital Hazards of Gambling and Adult Content

1. Stokel-Walker, C. (2024, December 27). People who visit adult or gambling websites double their risk of malware. *Fast Company.* https://www.fastcompany.com/91247694/people-who-visit-adult-or-gambling-websites-double-their-risk-of-malware.

2. Sivesind, C. (2024, September 12). The high stakes of cybersecurity in online gambling. *Secure World.* https://www.secureworld.io/industry-news/online-gambling-cybersecurity.
3. Trend Micro. (2025, January 22). Pop-up ads and fake warnings: How to spot and avoid it. *Trend Micro Help Center.* https://helpcenter.trendmicro.com/en-us/article/tmka-05037.
4. Clark, S. (2024, January 22). Experts say increased access to online gambling may put teens at risk. *University of Michigan Institute for Healthcare Policy & Innovation.* https://ihpi.umich.edu/news-events/news/experts-say-increased-access-online-gambling-may-put-teens-risk.
5. Puig, A. (2019, May 2). Malware from illegal video streaming apps: What to know. *Federal Trade Commission Consumer Alerts.* https://consumer.ftc.gov/consumer-alerts/2019/05/malware-illegal-video-streaming-apps-what-know.
6. Naprys, E. (2025, March 7). "Free" movie streams expose a million pirates to malware and data theft. *Cybernews.* https://cybernews.com/security/pirates-targeted-by-hackers-microsoft-warns/.
7. Hamzah, A. (2024, February 8). Users of illegal streaming websites, Android TV boxes face higher risk of malware, scams: Study. *The Star.* https://www.thestar.com.my/aseanplus/aseanplus-news/2024/02/08/users-of-illegal-streaming-websites-android-tv-boxes-face-higher-risk-of-malware-scams-study.
8. Doffman, Z. (2024, November 25). New Android 'dangerous' app warning—Change your phone settings now. *Forbes.* https://www.forbes.com/sites/zakdoffman/2024/11/25/new-android-dangerous-app-warning-check-your-phone-now/.

Part 10: Navigating the Maze of AI Scams

1. *Reuters.* (2025, March 19). Europol warns of AI-driven crime threats. https://www.reuters.com/world/europe/europol-warns-ai-driven-crime-threats-2025-03-18/.
2. Bisht, M. (2024, September 22). Mind games: How hackers exploit human psychology in phishing and social engineering. *LinkedIn.* https://www.linkedin.com/pulse/mind-games-how-hackers-exploit-human-psychology-phishing-bisht-ars9c.

3. *New York University.* (n.d.). AI-assisted cyberattacks and scams. https://www.nyu.edu/life/information-technology/safe-computing/protect-against-cybercrime/ai-assisted-cyberattacks-and-scams.html.
4. Gold, H. (2025, March 8). Celebrity AI deepfakes are flooding the internet. Hollywood is pushing Congress to fight back. *CNN.* https://edition.cnn.com/2025/03/08/tech/hollywood-celebrity-deepfakes-congress-law/index.html.
5. Pollina, R. (2024, October 18). Scammers swindle elderly California man out of $25K by using AI voice technology to claim his son was in "horrible accident," needed money for bail: "Absolutely his voice." *New York Post.* https://nypost.com/2024/10/18/us-news/scammers-swindle-elderly-california-man-out-of-25k-by-using-ai-voice-technology-to-claim-his-son-was-in-horrible-accident-needed-money-for-bail-absolutely-his-voice/.
6. Commodity Futures Trading Commission. (2024, January 25). CFTC customer advisory cautions the public to beware of artificial intelligence scams. https://www.cftc.gov/PressRoom/PressReleases/8854-24.
7. *Federal Trade Commission.* (2024, August 14). Federal Trade Commission announces final rule banning fake reviews and testimonials. https://www.ftc.gov/news-events/news/press-releases/2024/08/federal-trade-commission-announces-final-rule-banning-fake-reviews-testimonials.
8. Bal, A. (2024, July 7). The psychology of cyber fraud: How scammers use AI to exploit human behaviour. *International Journal of Creative Research Thoughts.* https://ijcrt.org/papers/IJCRT2407696.pdf.
9. Beh, M. T. (2025, March 19). Combating scam syndicates in Malaysia and Southeast Asia. Penang Institute. https://penanginstitute.org/publications/issues/combating-scam-syndicates-in-malaysia-and-southeast-asia.
10. *U.S. Department of the Treasury.* (2024, March 27). U.S. Department of the Treasury releases report on managing artificial intelligence-specific cybersecurity risks in the financial sector. https://home.treasury.gov/news/press-releases/jy2212.
11. Tan, E. J. (2025, February 24). Awareness: Online scams surge but awareness remains low. *The Edge Malaysia.* https://theedgemalaysia.com/node/745232.

LET THIS BOOK TRAVEL — *SHARE & PROTECT*

This book was made for everyone — and its true value begins when it moves beyond your hands.

If it gave you a new perspective, a sense of clarity, or simply made you pause and reflect — imagine what it might mean to someone else. Maybe a parent, a colleague, a student, or a friend who hasn't yet found the words to ask for help. Sometimes, a quiet reminder in the form of a book is all it takes to spark awareness and protect someone from unseen danger.

Every person who receives this book becomes part of something bigger. A shared effort. A quiet movement. Not led by institutions — but by individuals who care enough to pass it on. Each time it's shared, it carries not just knowledge, but kindness, protection, and hope.

That's why Lukas created this — not just as a book, but as a gesture. A small, human way to remind each other that we're not alone, and that we have the power to look out for one another.

Let this book speak again. Let it travel.

From hand to hand. From heart to heart.

Together, let's build a chain of protection.

Ts. Lukas J. Tan

WHO THIS BOOK HAS REACHED

Date	Given To	From (Name)	Notes of Wishes

ABOUT THE AUTHOR

Ts. Lukas J. Tan is a visionary entrepreneur, certified digital strategist, and cybersecurity advocate with over **two decades** of experience shaping Malaysia's digital landscape. As the founder of OPERiON, he leads a technology company that builds secure, scalable digital solutions for businesses, government, and civil society. Appointed as a National Industry Expert under the Jabatan Pembangunan Kemahiran (JPK), he has contributed to national policy efforts such as the *National Competency Standard Industry Forward (NCS-023:2025)*. Lukas has also served as a lecturer in computer science and regularly advises universities, reflecting his belief in bridging academia and industry to develop future-ready talent.

Beyond business, Lukas plays an active role in strengthening the national digital ecosystem. Through his *Waspada Penipuan Digital* campaign, he has delivered scam awareness education across schools in support of Jabatan Pendidikan Negeri Pulau Pinang. His initiatives have empowered thousands of students and SMEs to navigate digital threats confidently. As organising chairman of the *Penang Digitalisation Conference & Exhibition (PDX2025)*, he hosted panel discussions with national bodies including MCMC, CyberSecurity Malaysia, and Digital Penang—bringing together diverse stakeholders to raise awareness on cybersecurity, AI risks, and digital governance. For more, visit *www.lukastan.com*.

TO THOSE BEHIND THE SCREEN, THIS MOMENT IS YOURS

This isn't a warning or a lesson. It's simply a moment.

A moment to breathe. To reflect. To remember that there's more in you than this.

Maybe you started with curiosity. Or you followed someone's lead. Maybe you got good at it — and that skill gave you power.

But deep inside, a different part of you knows: you were meant for something greater.

Your ability to think, build, and influence — it's not a curse. It's a rare gift.

And gifts, when used with purpose, leave behind light.

You're not here by accident. Maybe this book found you for a reason.

Maybe this is the sign. The pause. The spark.

The path forward won't ask you to forget your past.

It only asks you to see it — and then rise from it.

You've seen how a single action can change someone's life.

Now imagine using that same power to protect, connect, and create.

No force is stronger than a person who wakes up and says:

"I choose to build something real."

And if that voice is yours — the world will feel it.

And many will be grateful you turned around.

- Ts. Lukas J. Tan

www.ingramcontent.com/pod-product-compliance
Lightning Source LLC
Chambersburg PA
CBHW041302210926
51847CB00010B/117
* 9 7 8 6 2 9 7 8 0 9 0 1 4 *